Holiday Hoopla: Multicultural Folk Tales

by Kathy Darling
illustrated by Marilynn G. Barr

Publisher: Roberta Suid
Copy Editor: Carol Whiteley
Design and Production: Susan Pinkerton
Cover Design: David Hale

Other books by the author in the Holiday Hoopla series:
Songs and Finger Plays; Flannel Board Fun;
Plays, Parades, Parties; and
Multicultural Celebrations

Entire contents copyright ©1994 by Monday Morning Books, Inc.,
Box 1680, Palo Alto, California 94302

For a complete catalog, please write to the address above.

monday morning.

Monday Morning is a registered trademark of
Monday Morning Books, Inc.

ISBN 1-878279-74-2

Printed in the United States of America
9 8 7 6 5 4 3 2 1

CONTENTS

INTRODUCTION   4

THE BOY WHO BREAKS CORN ROCK   5

THREE POOR SISTERS   17

BUDDHA CALLS THE ANIMALS   29

TWO LITTLE LEPRECHAUN SHOEMAKERS   45

THE ELEPHANT'S SURPRISE   57

PRINCESS PARSLEY   69

A THOUSAND LIGHTS FOR A KING   81

LITTLE JACK'S LANTERN   91

THE QUEEN OF HEARTS HAS A BIRTHDAY!   103

THE WISE BOY AND HIS DONKEY   115

RESOURCES   127

INTRODUCTION

Holiday Hoopla: Multicultural Folk Tales contains ten different folk tales from around the world. Each story offers many opportunities for audience participation, often with refrains for the children to repeat, as well as movements to mimic and lines to act out. The tales are followed by a variety of activities to extend the themes into several areas of the curriculum. Story-related patterns are also provided, with ideas for their use.

Each story is accompanied by a "Link into Literature" section. Here you'll find suggestions of books to read that will help broaden the children's cultural experiences. Some are popular folk tale picture books from the same country as the folk tale under study, and some relate similar tales from other lands. For instance, "The Boy Who Breaks Corn Rock" is a Mexican/Central American folk tale about the discovery of maize. The "Link into Literature" section in this unit lists six creation myths from other cultures.

The first time that each character or object appears in the stories, the word is written in boldface. This will make it easier for you to manipulate those patterns. The story-theme patterns may be used in many different ways, and how you choose to use them is up to you. You can trace the patterns onto felt, cut them out, decorate them, and use them on a traditional flannel board. Or you can color the paper patterns and back them with flannel pieces. The patterns can be used in simple puppet shows by gluing them onto Popsicle sticks and standing them in a sand table when they appear in the tale. Copies of the patterns can also be pasted onto extra large construction paper for a class "Big Book." Or you can dream up your own way to use them—one preschool teacher wears a big felt apron and uses felt patterns to tell the story right on the front. She walks about the room to give all the children a closer look at the characters—and they love it!

So have fun exploring the world of folk tales. Work with the activities provided, and encourage the children to discuss their own heritage. The wonderful folk tales told here may lead the children to relate some of their own favorites that are told at home.

THE BOY WHO BREAKS CORN ROCK
A Mexican/Central American Legend

Once there was a great **rock**.
It looked like a plain old rock, but it wasn't.
It was filled with tasty yellow **corn**.
Although the people of the village were hungry,
Nobody knew about the corn.
Then one day, **Fox** was smacking his lips when a **man** walked by.
"Well, excuse you!" the man said.
"What have you eaten that makes you smack your lips so loud?"
"Tasty golden kernels that the ants drop," said Fox.
"The corn is hidden in that great rock."
"Our people are so hungry," said the man.
"We must find these golden kernels."
He and Fox sat and watched the **ants** going by.
The ants go marching—they don't stop—hurrah, hurrah.
The ants go marching—they don't stop—hurrah, hurrah.
The ants go marching—they don't stop—
Not one kernel of corn is dropped—
And the ants go marching on.

Since no corn kernels were dropped,
The man thought Fox was lying and he went away.
But the next day, out came an ant with a kernel on its back.
The **kernel** dropped to the ground near Fox.
He tasted it, and smacked his lips.
"Well, excuse you," said the same man, who was passing by just
   then.
"Won't you tell me what makes you smack your lips so loud?"
Fox said, "Believe me, it is the kernels hidden in the great rock."
So the man waited again.
He sat and watched the ants going by.
The ants go marching—they don't stop—hurrah, hurrah.
The ants go marching—they don't stop—hurrah, hurrah.
The ants go marching—they don't stop—
Not one kernel of corn is dropped—
And the ants go marching on.

"We must call the Thunderboys," said the man.
"They will uncover the golden kernels."
The powerful Boys of Thunder came down from the heavens.
Fox smacked his lips loudly as he told about the kernels.

"So tasty, so tender, so sweet!" he said
"But where are the kernels?" asked the Boys of Thunder.
Fox pointed to the rock.
And the Thunderboys watched the rock.
The ants go marching—they don't stop—hurrah, hurrah.
The ants go marching—they don't stop—hurrah, hurrah.
The ants go marching—they don't stop—
Not one kernel of corn is dropped—
And the ants go marching on.

Now the **villagers** had gathered.
They begged the Thunderboys to find the tasty kernels.
The **first Thunderboy** stepped up.
"Thunder, thunder, crack the rock, tasty kernels all for me!"
He threw a great **thunderbolt**, but nothing happened.
"Oh, the rock is too big!" he cried.
The **second Thunderboy** stepped up.
"Thunder, thunder, crack the rock, tasty kernels all for me!"
And he threw a great thunderbolt, but nothing happened.
"Oh, the rock is too thick!" he cried.
The **third Thunderboy** stepped up.
"Thunder, thunder, crack the rock, tasty kernels all for me!"
And he threw a great thunderbolt, but again, nothing happened.
"Oh, the rock is too hard!" he cried.
"But we must have the kernels," the villagers cried.
"The rock is just too big," said the first Thunderboy.
"The rock is just too thick," said the second Thunderboy.
"The rock is just too hard," said the third Thunderboy.
The **fourth Thunderboy** was the last to speak.
He said, "The rock is just as big and thick and hard as it's going to be.
But all the people need tasty golden kernels."
So he stepped up to the rock and took a deep breath.
"Thunder, thunder, crack the rock,
Golden kernels for everyone to eat!"
And he threw a great thunderbolt that broke the rock in two.
Wonderful golden corn spilled out from the rock.
The Thunderboy made sure that everyone had plenty of corn.
Fox had a big dish—and he smacked his lips after every bite!

GET INTO THE ACT

✦ Let the children practice the refrain so they can sing the ant verse when it appears in the story. Invite small groups of children to stand in a line and sing the refrain:

The ants go marching—they don't stop—hurrah, hurrah.
The ants go marching—they don't stop—hurrah, hurrah.
The ants go marching—they don't stop—
Not one kernel of corn is dropped—
And the ants go marching on.

Children can march in place as they sing.

✦ Each time a thunderbolt is thrown, have the group clap together.

LINK INTO LEARNING

Tree-rific
Combine this story with a harvest celebration. Bring in a small living tree to decorate in a way that represents the harvest season.

Thunderbolt Board
1. Glue the rock pattern to the center of the bulletin board.
2. Let the children glue on kernels of unpopped corn below the rock (so that the kernels are "spilling" from the rock).
3. Give a thunderbolt pattern to each child to color. The children may want to coat their thunderbolts with glue and sprinkle with silver glitter.
4. Let the children glue or pin their finished thunderbolts on the bulletin board around the split "corn rock."

Option: Let children decorate the Thunderboy patterns to glue to the four corners of the board.

LINK INTO LITERATURE

This is an excellent time to introduce the children to creation myths found in cultures around the world. The following list includes stories from North American Indian tribes, West Africa, South America, and more.

✦ *Coyote Places the Stars* by Harriet Peck Taylor (Bradbury Press, 1993).

✦ *Rainbow Crow* by Nancy Van Laan (Alfred A. Knopf, 1989).

✦ *And God Created Squash* by Martha Whitmore Hickman (Albert Whitman, 1993).

✦ *The Woman Who Fell from the Sky* by John Bierhorst (William Morrow, 1993).

✦ *Moon Was Tired of Walking on Air* by Natalia M. Belting (Houghton Mifflin, 1992).

✦ *The Fire Children* by Eric Maddern (Dial, 1993).

THINK ABOUT IT!

Ask the children why they think that the first three Thunderboys failed to open the rock. What was different about what the fourth Thunderboy said as he threw his thunderbolt?

THE BOY WHO BREAKS CORN ROCK
Patterns

Rock

Ants

Corn Kernel   Corn Kernels

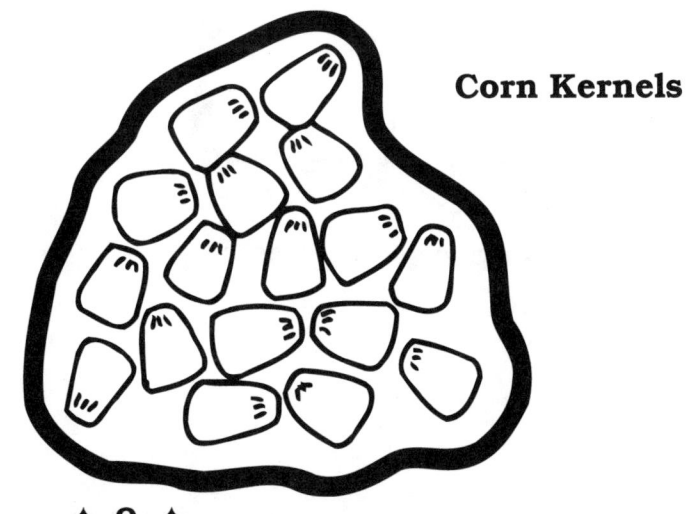

♦ 9 ♦

THE BOY WHO BREAKS CORN ROCK
Patterns

Man

Fox

THE BOY WHO BREAKS CORN ROCK
Pattern

Villagers

THE BOY WHO BREAKS CORN ROCK
Pattern

Thunderboy 1

THE BOY WHO BREAKS CORN ROCK
Pattern

Thunderboy 2

THE BOY WHO BREAKS CORN ROCK
Pattern

Thunderboy 3

THE BOY WHO BREAKS CORN ROCK
Pattern

Thunderboy 4

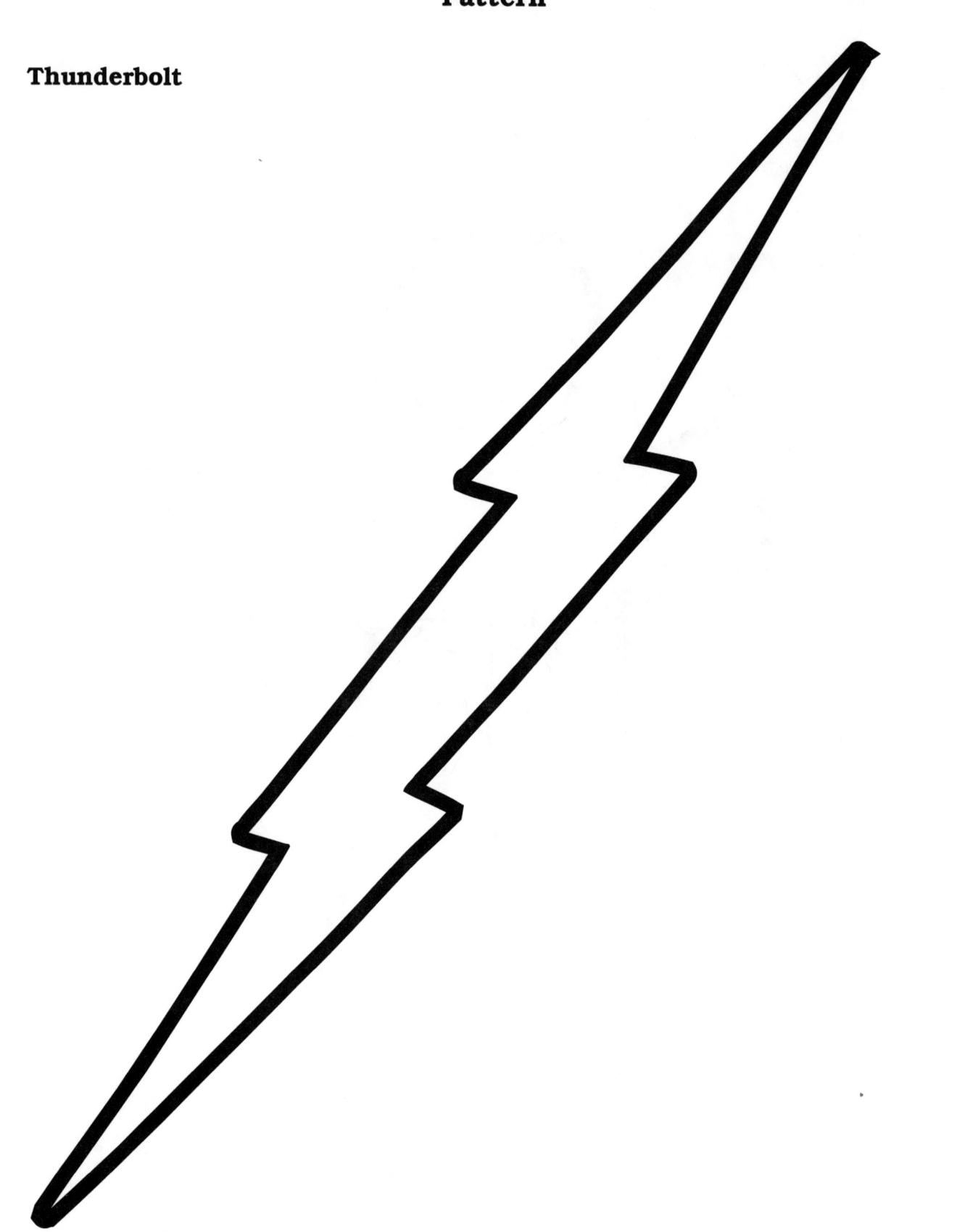

THE BOY WHO BREAKS CORN ROCK
Pattern

Thunderbolt

THREE POOR SISTERS
A Christmas Story Adapted from a Northern European Folk Tale

Once upon a time, a long time ago,
Three poor sisters lived in a little **cottage**
That had a very **squeaky door**.
The door would squeak whenever the sisters opened it.
"Squeak!" as they went out to the barn in the morning.
"Squeak!" as they went to the baker's for bread.
"Squeak!" as they went out to the garden at night.

The sisters didn't have much money,
But they were happy because they had each other.
Each morning they would milk their little **cow**.
Each afternoon they would walk to the **baker**
To buy a loaf of bread.
And each night they would pick **beans**
From the garden for their dinner.
And their door would squeak whenever they opened it.
"Squeak!" as they went out to the barn in the morning.
"Squeak!" as they went to the baker's for bread.
"Squeak!" as they went out to the garden at night.

Every morning was the same.
"It's time to milk the cow!" the **youngest sister** said.
Every afternoon was the same.
"It's time to go to the baker's!" the **middle sister** said.
Every evening was the same.
"It's time to pick the beans!" the **oldest sister** said.
And so it went from day to day.
There wasn't a penny left over—
Not a penny for a cake, not a penny for a candle.
There wasn't even a penny to buy oil
For the squeaky hinge on the door that went
"Squeak!" as they went out to the barn in the morning.
"Squeak!" as they went to the baker's for bread.
"Squeak!" as they went out to the garden at night.

Well, Christmas was coming and it filled the sisters with joy.
But they had no money for gifts.
They hoped that the baker might sprinkle a little sugar on their bread,
Or add raisins or nuts to the dough.

Now, this was long, long ago
And **Santa Claus** had just begun his trick of delivering gifts.
His beard was still short, and his tummy was still thin.
And when he came to a house,
He walked through the door like everyone else.
But the three poor sisters changed that.
On Christmas Eve they went to sleep as usual.
Santa had heard about these three poor sisters,
And this year he decided to visit their part of the world.
But when he came to their door and gave it a push
It went, "SQUEAK!"
The three sisters rustled in their beds.
Santa thought of a way he could get in without waking them.
He climbed to the roof and slid down the **chimney**,
And that's how he's done it ever since!
For each sister Santa left a sugar cake, a candle,
And a big **bag of gold**!
On Christmas morning the sisters were very surprised!
The very first thing they did with their shiny new coins
Was to fix the squeaky door!
So the next time you're wondering why Santa comes down chimneys,
Instead of using the door like everyone else,
Think of the three poor sisters and how it all started!

GET INTO THE ACT

✦ Let the children squeak along with the door on the refrain:
"Squeak!" as they went out to the barn in the morning.
"Squeak!" as they went to the baker's for bread.
"Squeak!" as they went out to the garden at night.

LINK INTO LEARNING

Bags of Gold
1. Cut several bags of "gold" from heavy yellow paper.
2. Mark the back of each with a number from one to five.
3. Have the children glue on the correct number of "pennies" (cut from copper or brown paper) to match the numeral on each bag.

Sorting Change
Let the children practice sorting real coins into nickels, dimes, etc., or have them stack coins in piles of five.

Santa's New Route
1. Make a copy of the chimney and Santa patterns for each child.
2. Have the children color the patterns.
3. Give the children paper and crayons to draw a house with a squeaky door.
4. Let the children glue chimneys to the roofs and then place their Santas in the pictures. Will Santa slide down the chimney or go through the squeaky door?

The Cottage of the Three Sisters
1. Let the children color in the three poor sisters patterns.
2. Give the children shoe boxes or shirt boxes to use for cottages. They can look through home-theme magazines for furniture and other effects to cut out and glue to the interior.
3. Encourage the children to place the three sisters in their cottage.
4. Set up a small village with all the cottage scenes.

LINK INTO LITERATURE

✦ *The Legend of Old Befana* by Tomi de Paola (Harcourt Brace, 1980). This picture book tells the story of how Old Befana went looking for the "Child King." Even though she never found him, Befana continues to fly through the sky on Twelfth Night, leaving gifts for children around the world.

✦ *The Polar Bear Express* by Edward Packard (Bantam Books, 1984). This beautifully illustrated book will take children on a magical journey that happened one Christmas night.

✦ *The Night Before Christmas* by Mike Artell (Alladin, 1994). The bright illustrations in this version of the classic tale are perfect for preschoolers.

THINK ABOUT IT!

The three sisters were poor, but happy. Ask the children why they think the sisters were happy. (Possible answers: because they had each other, because they had everything they needed—food, shelter, friends.)

Ask the children what things make them happy.

THREE POOR SISTERS
Patterns

Youngest Sister

Middle Sister

THREE POOR SISTERS
Patterns

Santa Claus

Oldest Sister

THREE POOR SISTERS
Pattern

Cottage

THREE POOR SISTERS
Pattern

Squeaky Door

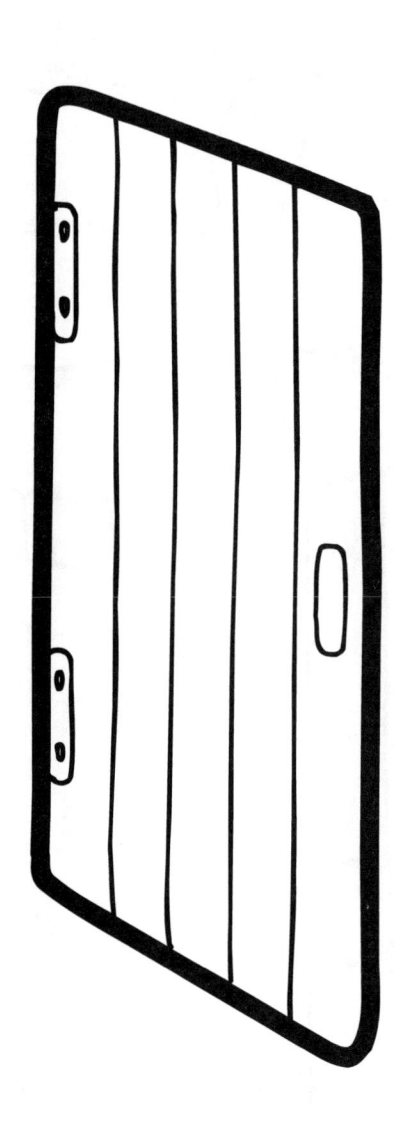

THREE POOR SISTERS
Pattern

Cow

THREE POOR SISTERS
Pattern

Baker

THREE POOR SISTERS
Pattern

Beans

THREE POOR SISTERS
Patterns

Chimney   Bag of Gold

BUDDHA CALLS THE ANIMALS
A Story of the Twelve Animals of the Chinese Zodiac

One day, a long time ago,
Buddha decided that he wanted to see
All of the animals in the world.
There were so many animals to tell,
It would take a very long time to reach them all.
And because **Rat** was busiest at this time of night,
Always scurrying about anyway,
He was given the job of messenger.
Rat was to begin that very night, at the stroke of twelve.
First, Rat went out to the villages and into the farms.
He whispered to **Ox**, who was slow-moving
    and would need some time,
"Buddha calls, come at once."

Then he left the villages and he came to **Tiger**,
"Buddha calls, come at once."

To **Rabbit** in his burrow, Rat squeaked,
"Buddha calls, come at once."

Rat was nervous as he approached the water.
Tip-toeing near, he called,
"All fishes! All fishes of the sea,
Buddha calls, come at once."

No fish answered, but great **Dragon** poked up his head.
"What is it?!" he boomed powerfully. "Buddha calls?"
Rat scurried away, telling **Snake** as he passed,
"Buddha calls, come at once!"

Rat scampered past a country home, telling **Horse** and **Sheep**,
"Buddha calls, come at once!"

Then he walked through the forest, looking for more animals.
To **Monkey**, swinging in the tree, he said,
"Buddha calls, come at once."

To the birds in the trees, he called,
"Buddha calls, come at once!"

But they simply fluttered about.
Rat ran back toward the village,
He was beginning to get tired.
He passed one last farm, and there he called
To **Rooster**, and **Dog**, and **Pig**,
"Buddha calls, come at once!

*Come, come now, day begins to break
And Buddha wishes to see us all!"*
He passed Cat sleeping under a bush.
"Wake up, Cat! Buddha calls, come at once."

But Cat just purred, "I prefer to sleep."
When the sun came out bright and bold,
All the animals stood before Buddha—
But not all the animals of the kingdom!
Rat and Ox and Tiger and Rabbit were there.
But the fishes must not have heard.
Dragon was there, powerful and proud.
Snake had slithered up, and Horse and Sheep had come, too.
Monkey was awake and present,
But the birds were missing.
Rooster, Dog, and Pig had come, but Cat preferred to sleep.
Buddha was very pleased that these twelve had arrived,
When all other animals had ignored his call.
Buddha gave these animals a special gift.
He named a year in the Chinese calendar after each of them!
Each would get to be the special animal for a whole year,
And that new year would begin with a big parade.
After each of them had taken a turn being the animal of the year,
Their turns would start over again!
And Rat, the busy little midnight messenger, was the first!

GET INTO THE ACT

✦ Let students recite Rat's call each time he comes to a new animal: *"Buddha calls, come at once!"*

LINK INTO LEARNING

Buddha's Bulletin Board
1. On the chalk board or bulletin board, display in a line the twelve animals in the order they appear in the story.
2. Give each child a long piece of construction paper or butcher paper and a copy of the animal patterns.
3. Let the children color the animal patterns and then glue them onto their papers in the correct sequence, using your display as a guide.

There's a Monkey on My Back!
1. Fasten a paper animal to each child's back, without telling what the animal is.
2. Let the children walk around the room looking at each other's tags.
3. Encourage the children to help each other guess their animal by giving sound hints. Example: If one child is wearing a dog pattern, other children can bark, pant, or beg. If a child is wearing the snake, other children can hiss, slither, or flick out their tongue.

Animal Charades
1. Place all of the animal patterns in a bag.
2. Ask a child to come up and reach into the bag for a pattern.
3. Have the child look at the chosen animal, and then act it out so the group can guess it.
4. The first child to guess correctly can act out the next animal.

Cooperative Chinese Zodiac (for groups of 12 children)
1. Cut a large circle from a piece of construction paper and mark twelve years around the outer edge, starting with the present year and working backward.
2. Cut a smaller circle from another color of paper, glue it to the center of the first, and write "Our Classroom Zodiac" on it.
3. Give each child a different animal pattern to color.
4. Let the children help glue these onto the outer edge of the second circle, under the correct year (see the patterns for year-animal information).

LINK INTO LITERATURE

✦ *Why Rat Comes First: A Story of the Chinese Zodiac* by Clara Yen (Children's Book Press, 1991). This book provides a great opportunity for your children to make some literary comparisons! Encourage them to try and identify how the stories and illustrations differ. Which do they like better? Which animals are their favorites?

Two more books on Chinese culture (although not about the zodiac) are:

✦ *Two of Everything* by Lily Toy Hong (Albert Whitman, 1993).

✦ *Chinese Mother Goose Rhymes* selected and edited by Robert Wyndham (Philomel, 1989).

THINK ABOUT IT!

Ask the children why they think the fish didn't come when Buddha called. If any of the students have fish for pets, ask them if it's easy for fish to travel on their own. How are the fish in the story different from the cat? Would the cat have been able to visit Buddha if it had wanted to?

BUDDHA CALLS THE ANIMALS
Pattern

Buddha

BUDDHA CALLS THE ANIMALS
Patterns

Snake (1989)

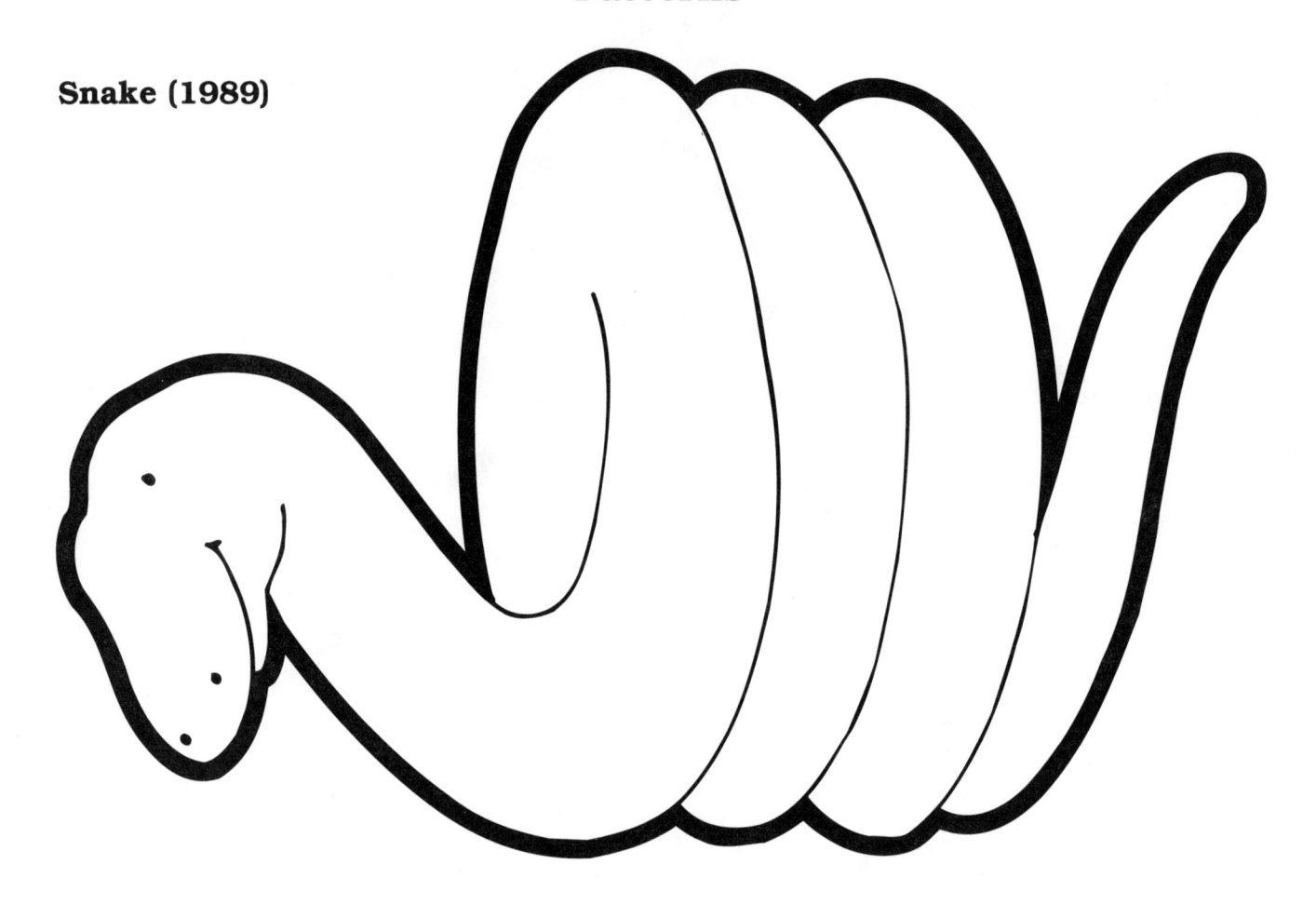

Rat (1984)

BUDDHA CALLS THE ANIMALS
Pattern

Ox (1985)

BUDDHA CALLS THE ANIMALS
Pattern

Tiger (1986)

BUDDHA CALLS THE ANIMALS
Pattern

Rabbit (1987)

BUDDHA CALLS THE ANIMALS
Pattern

Dragon (1988)

BUDDHA CALLS THE ANIMALS
Pattern

Horse (1990)

BUDDHA CALLS THE ANIMALS
Pattern

Sheep (1991)

BUDDHA CALLS THE ANIMALS
Pattern

Monkey (1992)

BUDDHA CALLS THE ANIMALS
Pattern

Rooster (1993)

BUDDHA CALLS THE ANIMALS
Pattern

Dog (1994)

BUDDHA CALLS THE ANIMALS
Pattern

Pig (1995)

TWO LITTLE LEPRECHAUN SHOEMAKERS
An Irish Folk Tale

Once upon a time in Ireland,
There lived two little leprechauns.
They were hard-working shoemakers,
And you could hear them working, deep in the forest.
"Tap, tap, tap," went their little **hammers**.
"Tap, tap, tap," on the **soles of the shoes**.

Still, they were poor little leprechauns,
And they needed to sell more shoes.
One of the leprechauns, named **Patrick**, was always in a hurry.
He said, "Faster, faster, make more shoes!"
But the other leprechaun, called **Jimmy**, was careful with his work.
He said, "Poor as I am, I take my time!"
For Jimmy made only the finest shoes,
And doing your best takes time.
"Tap, tap, tap," went their little hammers.
"Tap, tap, tap," on the soles of the shoes.

One day, Patrick looked out the **shoe shop** window
And saw a little **gnome** hop out of the forest.
The gnome knocked on the door very loudly.
Then he stepped inside and shouted,
"I'm going to be married today,
And I need wedding boots! I need them by noon!"
"Coming right up," said Patrick. "But you'll pay a fee!"
"It isn't possible," said Jimmy. "It just can't be!
Wedding boots will take hours to make
With the finest leather and the strongest stitches!"
The gnome went away without any boots.
Patrick grumbled,
But he kept on working just as he should.
"Tap, tap, tap," went their little hammers.
"Tap, tap, tap," on the soles of the shoes.

Some days later, a **man** pounded on the little door.
Patrick opened it wide and looked up
To see the man standing very tall.
"I need some little booties, this very night,
Soft little booties for my first-born son!"
"Coming right up," said Patrick. "But you'll pay a fee!"

♦ 45 ♦

"It isn't possible," said Jimmy. "It just can't be!
Why, baby booties would take days to make.
We'd have to send for the softest wool!"
The man went away without any booties.
Patrick grumbled,
But he kept on working just as he should.
"Tap, tap, tap," went their little hammers.
"Tap, tap, tap," on the soles of the shoes.

A little while later, a **fairy messenger** flew to their shop.
Her wings beat gently against the door.
"I need **dancing shoes** today," she told them,
"Dancing shoes for fairies, and a dozen pairs in all!"
"Coming right up," said Patrick. "But you'll pay a fee!"
"It isn't possible," said Jimmy. "It just can't be!
Why, dancing shoes would take weeks to make,
With the tiniest stitches on the softest satin!"
And the fairy went away without any dancing shoes.
Patrick grumbled,
But he kept on working just as he should.
"Tap, tap, tap," went their little hammers.
"Tap, tap, tap," on the soles of the shoes.

Well, the **Fairy Queen** was the one who needed those shoes.
They were to be worn by her own castle dancers!
When she heard Jimmy's reply, she sent the fairy back.
"I am willing to wait for the finest dancing shoes
Made with the tiniest stitches
On the softest satin!" was her reply.
And the queen was so pleased with the shoes when they arrived
That she made the two leprechauns her Official Shoemakers!
Patrick learned his lesson, and never hurried again,
Because if something is worth making,
It's worth making well.
And both kept on working just as they should.
"Tap, tap, tap," went their little hammers.
"Tap, tap, tap," on the soles of the shoes.

GET INTO THE ACT

✦ Let three children play the roles of the gnome, the man, and the fairy messenger, each giving the appropriate-sounding knocks on the door: loud rapping, pounding, and then the softest taps.

✦ Encourage all of the students to join in on the refrain:
"Tap, tap, tap," went their little hammers.
"Tap, tap, tap," on the soles of the shoes.

LINK INTO LEARNING

Shoe-making Fun
1. Let the children trace around their shoes onto heavy-duty art paper and then cut out.
2. Provide a variety of art materials for the children to use to decorate their shoe outlines, including: sequins, lace, colorful ribbons, fabric scraps, markers, crayons, glitter, and glue.
3. Encourage the children to create the most fantastic foot coverings ever—shoes that could be made only by one of the most talented leprechaun cobblers!

Whose Shoes?
1. With parents' permission, have the children bring in the funniest, prettiest, largest, or strangest shoe that they can find at home (it doesn't have to be their own).
2. Assemble the shoes in a display. Discuss who might wear each shoe. What might the person be doing while wearing the shoe?
3. Sort by color. Arrange by size.

Imaginary Fairy
1. Have the children think about all the different fairies they've heard of: the Tooth Fairy, Tinker Bell, Cinderella's fairy godmother, etc.
2. Then have them imagine their own fairy godmother (or godfather), and draw a picture of her or him.

LINK INTO LITERATURE

✦ *Jamie O'Rourke and the Big Potato* by Tomie de Paola (G. P. Putnam's Sons, 1992).
In this Irish tale, a lazy farmer grows the biggest potato ever seen. After reading this delightful story, have the children think of all the possible ways to eat potatoes: French fried, baked, mashed, boiled, etc.

✦ *Tim O'Tool and the Wee Folk* retold by Gerald McDermott (Viking, 1990).
This classic story is about a poor man named Tim who comes upon a group of partying leprechauns (or "wee folk"). They give him a series of gifts (a goose that lays golden eggs, a magic tablecloth, and an astounding hat) that change his luck forever.

✦ *Daniel O'Rourke* retold by Gerald McDermott (Viking, 1986).
Daniel O'Rourke dances, eats, and drinks too much at the party at the nearby mansion—and his dreams that night reflect his over-indulgences.

THINK ABOUT IT!

Ask the children what kinds of activities they take their time with: coloring, cutting, writing their names, and so on. Have the children consider whether it is okay to hurry when doing certain jobs. (Examples: firefighter, ambulance driver, police officer, etc.) Ask if they can think of what these jobs have in common. (Emergencies.)

TWO LITTLE LEPRECHAUN SHOEMAKERS
Patterns

Hammer

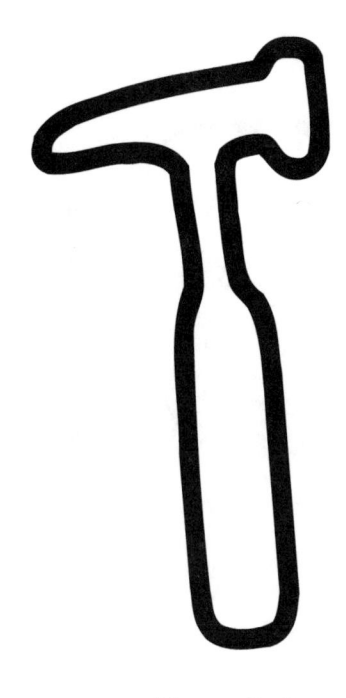

Shoe Sole

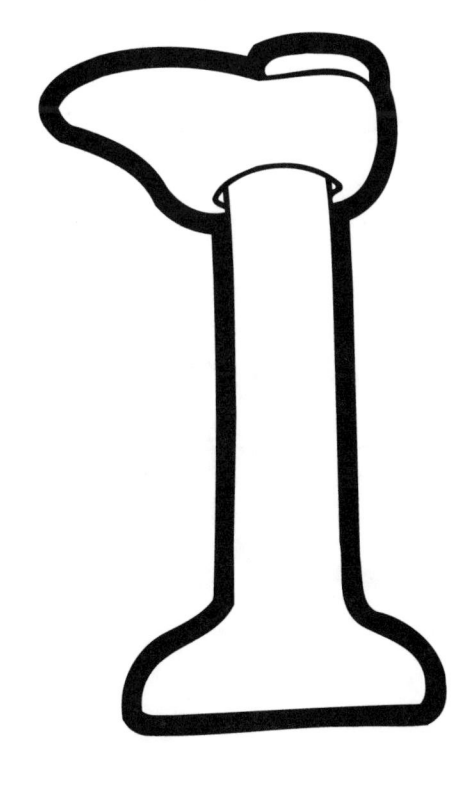

TWO LITTLE LEPRECHAUN SHOEMAKERS
Pattern

Patrick

TWO LITTLE LEPRECHAUN SHOEMAKERS
Pattern

Jimmy

TWO LITTLE LEPRECHAUN SHOEMAKERS
Pattern

Shoe Shop

TWO LITTLE LEPRECHAUN SHOEMAKERS
Pattern

Gnome

TWO LITTLE LEPRECHAUN SHOEMAKERS
Pattern

Man

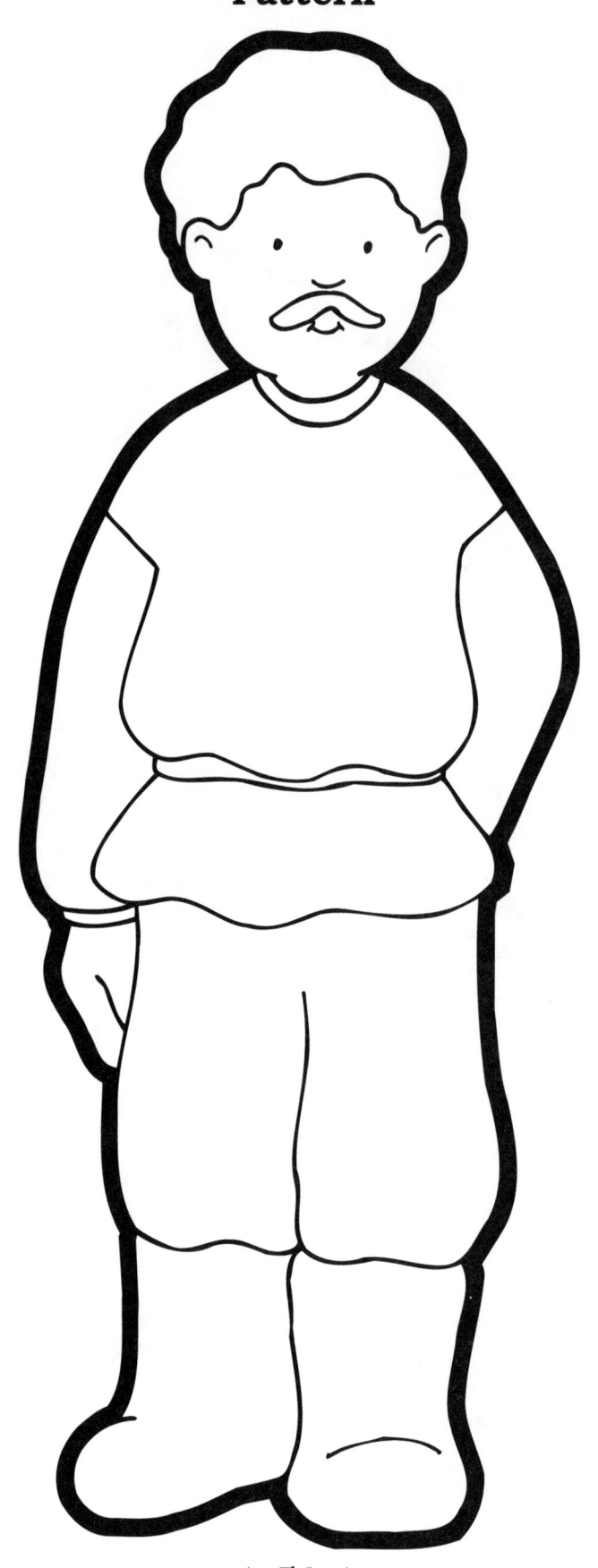

TWO LITTLE LEPRECHAUN SHOEMAKERS
Patterns

Fairy Messenger

Dancing Shoes

TWO LITTLE LEPRECHAUN SHOEMAKERS
Pattern

Fairy Queen

THE ELEPHANT'S SURPRISE
An African Folk Tale

Long ago, in Africa,
Elephants roamed the land in great numbers.
At any time you might hear a loud noise—
A clomping! A stomping!
A thomping shuffle of heavy . . . thumping . . . elephant feet!

And long ago there lived a family—a **mother** and her **three sons**.
They worked and played under the hot **sun**,
And they slept under the cool **moon**.
All day long they worked in their **pumpkin patch**,
Planting and caring for the vegetable vines.
It was dry and hot, but a cool river flowed by,
And the river helped water the fields.
With plenty of water and lots of hard work,
The family grew delicious pumpkins—juicy and round.
They grew **small yellow pumpkins,**
Medium-sized orange pumpkins,
And great, **huge pumpkins** as red as the sun.
When the mother needed tools, spices,
Baskets, or colorful cloth,
She loaded her pumpkins onto a big **cart**
And rolled them off to the village.
She traded the pumpkins for what she needed.
The mother served baked or mashed pumpkins
To feed her hungry boys,
And they grew strong and healthy.
All was well with this family
Until one warm, still night.
The mother and her boys slept deeply after working hard all day.
But when Sipho, the smallest and youngest, awoke in the morning,
He found a horrible sight!
Broken pumpkins were everywhere! Crushed pumpkins!
Bumped pumpkins! Lumpy pumpkins!
Sipho's oldest brother stayed awake all the next night,
Hoping to discover what had destroyed so many pumpkins.
He peeked through the brush at the side of the field,
When suddenly, he heard a loud, loud noise—
A clomping! A stomping!
A thomping shuffle of heavy . . . thumping . . . elephant feet!

The great big elephants trampled through,
Eating the pumpkins and tossing them about.
The boy woke up his mother right away.
"We must save our pumpkins!" she cried.
They stayed up the rest of the night, thinking of a plan.
"We must hide someone inside a huge pumpkin," the boy said.
"When the elephant swallows the pumpkin,
The person inside will tickle the elephant with a feather
And frighten it away!
But it must be someone small enough to fit inside a pumpkin."
The mother and the brother both looked at little Sipho.
At first, Sipho said, "No way!"
But his mother and brother convinced him.
So, the next morning, they hollowed out the juiciest pumpkin.
They gave Sipho special charms for luck and bravery,
And smeared him with slippery fat.
They handed him a tickling feather,
And gently put **Sipho in the pumpkin**.
Then they put him out in the field with the other pumpkins.
That night the elephants came . . .
A clomping! A stomping!
A thomping shuffle of heavy . . . thumping . . . elephant feet!

The **lead elephant** spotted the juicy pumpkin right away.
He swallowed it whole.
Sipho felt himself squish tight as he slid into the elephant's
    stomach.
But like a flash, Sipho held up his feather,
And tickled . . . and tickled . . . and tickled the elephant
Until the elephant finally sneezed in a fit.
Sipho flew out of his mouth, safe and sound!
And the elephants all ran away in fear and never came back!
Sipho's mother hugged and kissed him,
And the whole family cheered brave Sipho!
That night, many friends came to celebrate,
And the family was never again bothered by . . .
A clomping! A stomping!
A thomping shuffle of heavy . . . thumping . . . elephant feet!

GETTING INTO THE ACT

✦ Have the children sit on the floor, place their hands flat in front of them, and add sound effects to the story by slapping the floor on the following lines:

A clomping! A stomping!
A thomping shuffle of heavy . . . thumping . . . elephant feet!

✦ Give each child a pattern of each of the three pumpkins. Let the children color the pumpkins in the colors mentioned in the story (yellow, orange, and red). When you read the story again, have the children hold up the pumpkin that matches the one described.

LINK INTO LEARNING

Placing Pumpkins

1. Paste three colored pumpkin patterns (small yellow, medium-sized orange, and large red) onto empty oatmeal boxes or shoe boxes.
2. Have the children sort other pumpkin patterns by size and color and put them in the right boxes.

Lucky Charms

1. Sipho was given special charms for luck. Ask your children if they have any special charms or mementos that are important to them.
2. Have the children bring these items for show and tell.
3. Or let the children draw small objects (real or imagined) that are important to them.

Story Scene

Use a piece of wood for the base of this pumpkin-filled story scene.
1. Children can make a blue clay river to place on the base.
2. Pumpkins can be molded from yellow, orange, or red clay. Or the children can cut out circles of colored paper for the pumpkins.
3. Provide story patterns for the children to color and cut out. They may want to glue the patterns onto Popsicle sticks, press the sticks into balls of clay, and then set them about the scene.

LINK INTO LITERATURE

✦ *Bringing the Rain to Kapiti Plain* by Verna Aardeme (Dial, 1981). This is a lyrical story that tells how Ki-pat helps end the dry season. It is reminiscent of the rhyme "The House That Jack Built." Read both and see if children recognize the rhythm.

✦ *Where Are You Going, Manyoni?* by Catherine Stock (Morrow, 1993).
In this lovely picture book, set on the Limpopo River in Zimbabwe, a girl makes her way across the country to school one morning. The book illustrates the fact that people in different cultures often follow similar routines. It includes a wildlife guide that names the different animals appearing in the colorful pages.

THINK ABOUT IT!

Ask the children to think of other ways that Sipho and his family might have guarded their pumpkin patch from the elephants. Could they have built a fence? Made a scarecrow? Guarded the pumpkins night and day?

Sipho and his family lived primarily off pumpkins. Ask the children if they can think of one food (or type of food) that they could eat without getting tired of it.

THE ELEPHANT'S SURPRISE
Pattern

Elephants

THE ELEPHANT'S SURPRISE
Patterns

Mother

Cart of Pumpkins

THE ELEPHANT'S SURPRISE
Patterns

Oldest Boy

Middle Boy

THE ELEPHANT'S SURPRISE
Pattern

Sipho

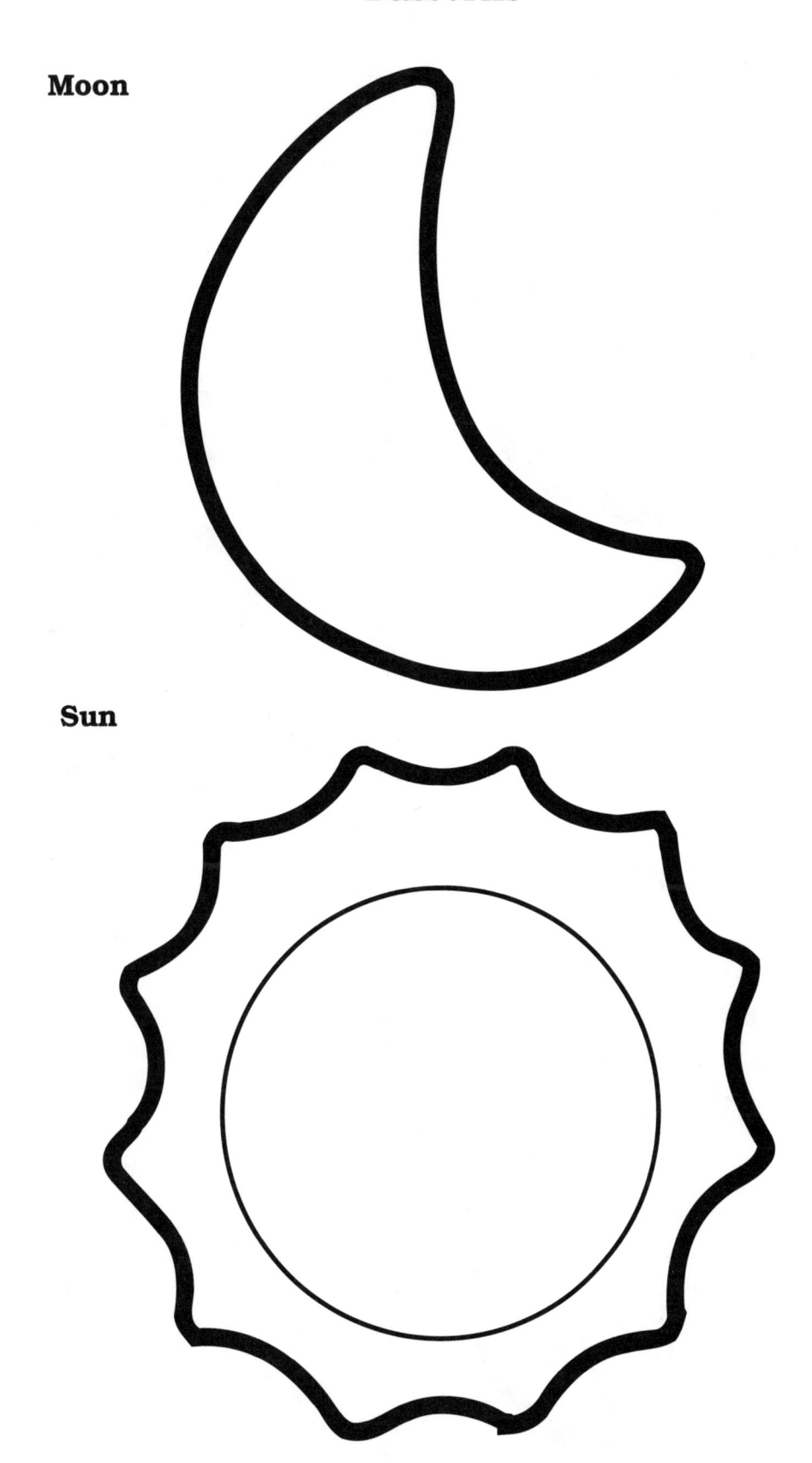

THE ELEPHANT'S SURPRISE
Patterns

Moon

Sun

THE ELEPHANT'S SURPRISE
Patterns

Small Pumpkin

Pumpkin Patch

Medium Pumpkin

THE ELEPHANT'S SURPRISE
Patterns

Pumpkin with Sipho

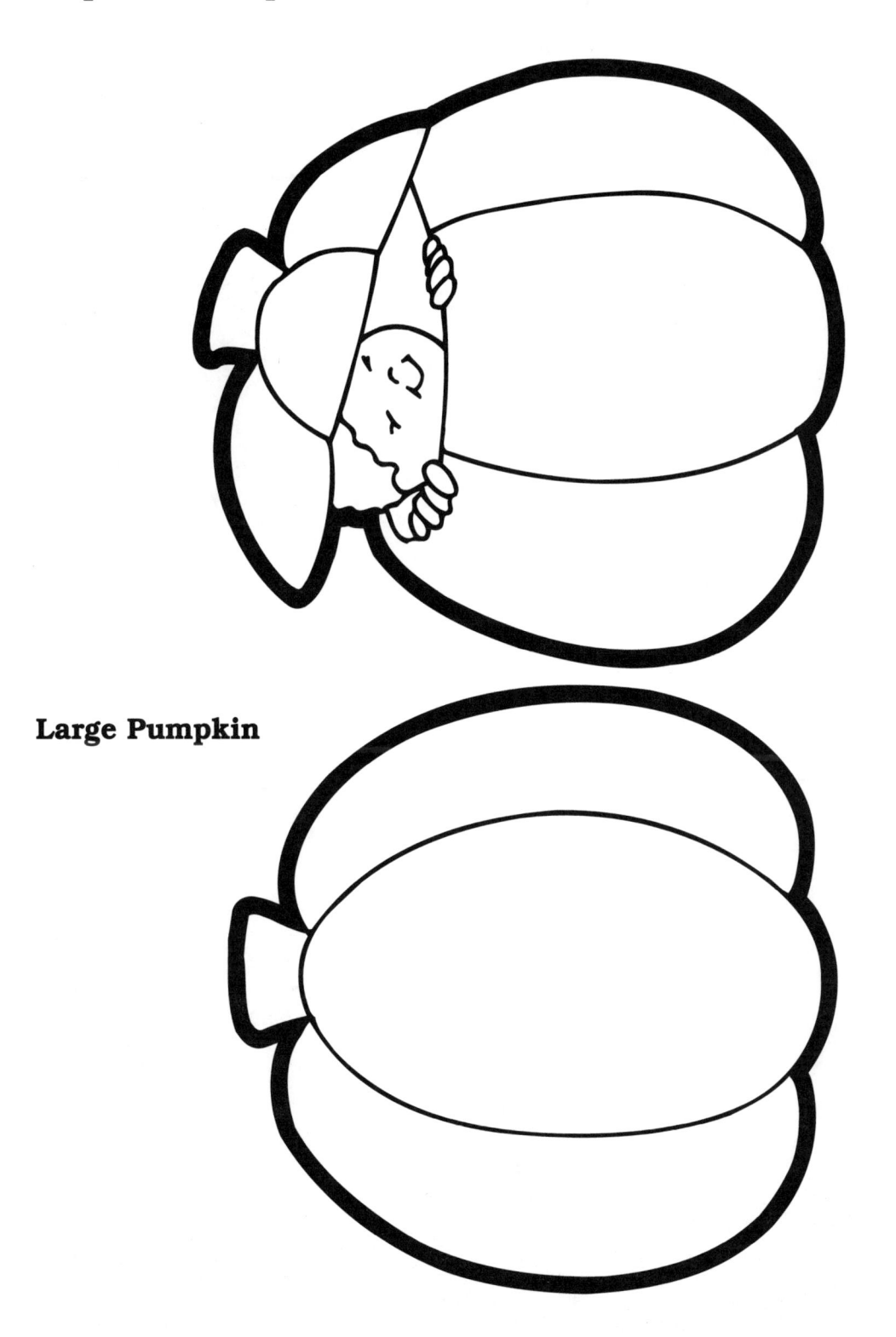

Large Pumpkin

THE ELEPHANT'S SURPRISE
Pattern

Lead Elephant

PRINCESS PARSLEY
A Japanese Tale

Once there was a **mother.**
Who lived with her **daughter**.
They were poor, but they were happy to have each other.
Every day, the daughter made parsley soup for dinner.
She walked up the **hill**
To pick the **parsley**.
She sang in the fields as she picked,
"Soup for my mother, and soup for me.
Picking all the parsley, 1-2-3!"

The villagers in her town gave her a nickname.
They called her Princess Parsley!
One day, while she was picking parsley,
She saw the **villagers** gathering on the road.
They seemed very excited, and they stopped to tell her,
"He's coming! He's coming!
The great Shotoku is coming!"
"Who is he?" the girl asked.
"He is the great Prince Shotoku," they told her.
"He is a fair and honest ruler."
The girl wanted to wait and see the prince go by,
But she knew her poor mother was waiting for the soup.
So she went back to the fields, bending to pick the parsley
And put it in her **basket**.
She sang as she picked,
"Soup for my mother, and soup for me.
Picking all the parsley, 1-2-3!
Picking all the parsley, 4-5-6!
*Put it in the **pot**, then mix, mix, mix!"*

Soon the **prince** paraded down the road.
He waved to the people and they waved back.
It seemed that everyone in the village was there watching,
Except for one girl on the hill,
Bending low to the ground, basket in arm.
The prince wondered why the girl didn't look up, or turn to see him go by.
He sent a **messenger** to ask her why she didn't join the villagers
And watch the parade.
The girl looked up in surprise.
"I'm sorry," she told the messenger.

"Please tell the prince to forgive me,
But my first duty is to my mother.
She is old and tired and wants parsley soup."
Then the princess bent low again, singing as she did,
"Soup for my mother, and soup for me.
Picking all the parsley, 1-2-3!
Picking all the parsley, 4-5-6!
Put it in the pot, then mix, mix, mix!"

The prince heard her answer, and was touched by the girl's kindness.
When he returned from his trip through the land,
He sent a messenger once again.
The messenger arrived at the girl's **hut**.
He told her that the prince wanted to meet her, and taste her soup.
She could hardly believe it! The prince was coming to her hut!
She rushed out of the door with her basket,
And she sang in the fields as she picked,
"Soup for my mother, and soup for me.
Picking all the parsley, 1-2-3!
Picking all the parsley, 4-5-6!
Put it in the pot, then mix, mix, mix!
Hurry! Hurry! 7-8-9!
The prince is coming to our hut to dine!"

That evening the prince arrived at dinner time.
He ate parsley soup with the woman and her daughter.
They talked all through the evening, while eating the parsley soup.
The prince thought the girl was as smart and beautiful as she was kind.
"May I marry your daughter?" he asked the old woman.
"You have my blessing," the old woman answered,
"But you should ask her yourself."
So the prince asked the girl, "Will you marry me?"
"Yes!" Princess Parsley said with a smile.
They were married soon after in the **castle**.
All of the villagers came to the wedding.
The prince built a **big house** near the castle for the mother,
And they planted parsley all around.

GET INTO THE ACT

✦ Divide the children into three groups. Give each group two lines to rehearse. Chant along with the children until they have learned their lines. Then let each group chant their lines when they appear in the story.

Group 1: *Soup for my mother, and soup for me,*
Picking all the parsley, 1-2-3!

Group 2: *Picking all the parsley, 4-5-6!*
Put it in the pot, then mix, mix, mix!

Group 3: *Hurry! Hurry! 7-8-9!*
The prince is coming to our hut to dine!

✦ Encourage the children to act out the lines, reaching out to pick the parsley, stirring a spoon in the pot, or hurrying (in place) up a hill.

LINK INTO LEARNING

Princess Parsley's Herb Garden
Parsley is easy to plant and grows abundantly.
1. Brainstorm the types of herbs and spices that the children's families use at home.
2. Buy parsley and other herb seedlings at a nursery, as well as soil.
3. Let the children prepare the soil and help plant the seedlings in containers.
4. Set up a watering schedule so that each child is responsible for helping the plants to grow.

Dramatic Diorama
1. Give each child a pattern of Princess Parsley and Prince Shotoku to color and decorate.
2. Distribute shoe boxes or larger cardboard boxes for the children to use to create dioramas.
3. If available, let the children use grass, leaves, twigs, and other natural materials to create a hillside scene before placing the characters in their box. Otherwise, provide colored construction paper and fabric scraps for the hillside.

LINK INTO LITERATURE

✦ *The Samurai's Daughter* by Robert D. San Souci (Dial, 1992). This beautifully illustrated book about a loyal Japanese daughter is well-suited for first and second graders. You may need to simplify for younger listeners.

✦ *Bamboo Hats and a Rice Cake* by Anne Tompert (Crown, 1993). Set at the time of the Japanese New Year, this tale includes the Japanese lettering for many objects mentioned in the story.

THINK ABOUT IT!

Princess Parsley helped her mother by making dinner every evening. Ask the children the following question: "Does anyone count on you at home?"

Have the children think about what types of chores they could do to lend a helping hand to the adults in their families. Examples: feeding a pet, keeping their room clean, setting the table, etc.

PRINCESS PARSLEY
Patterns

Mother

Princess Parsley

PRINCESS PARSLEY
Pattern

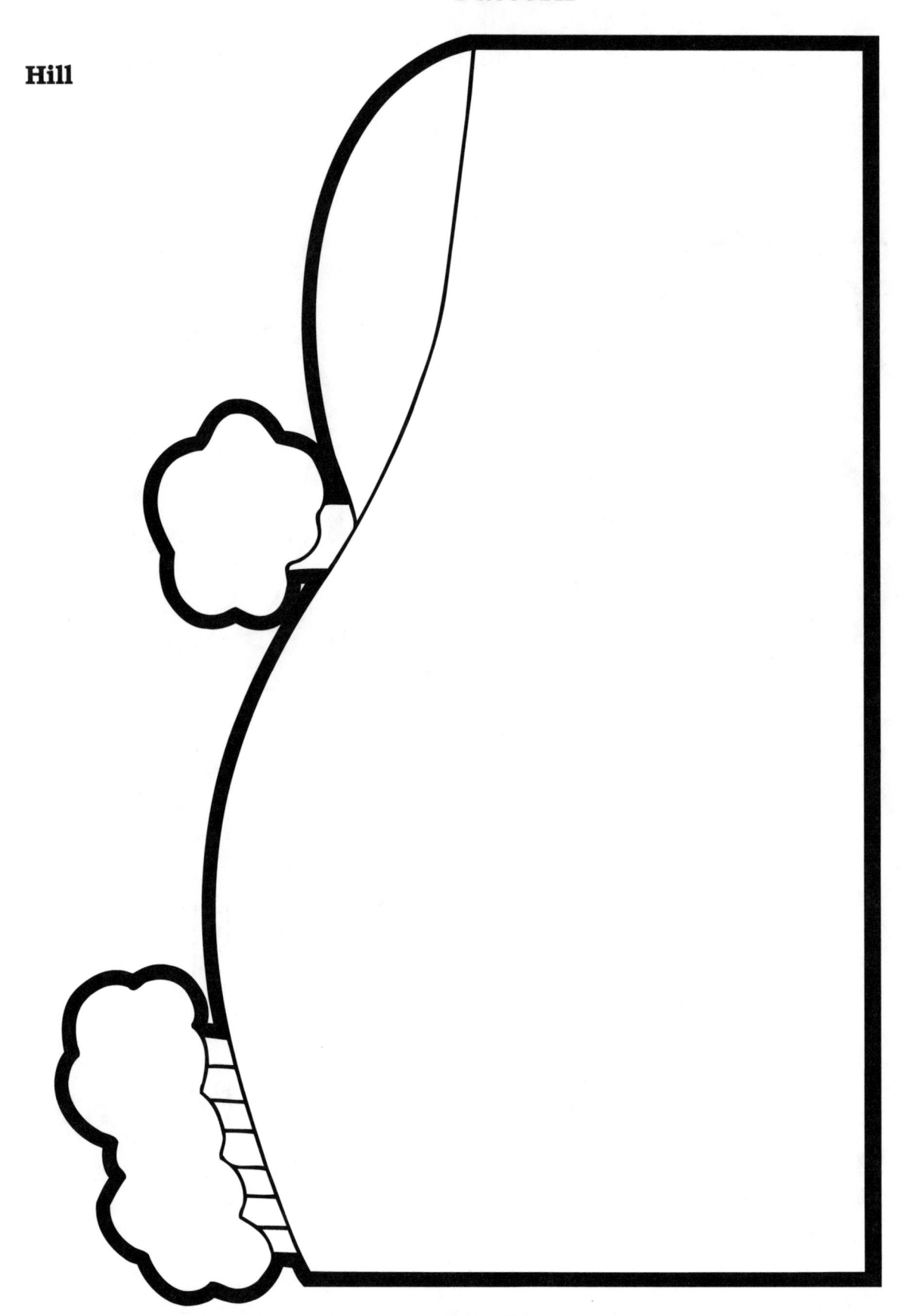

Hill

PRINCESS PARSLEY
Pattern

Villagers

PRINCESS PARSLEY
Patterns

Basket

Parsley

Pot

PRINCESS PARSLEY
Patterns

Shotoku

Messenger

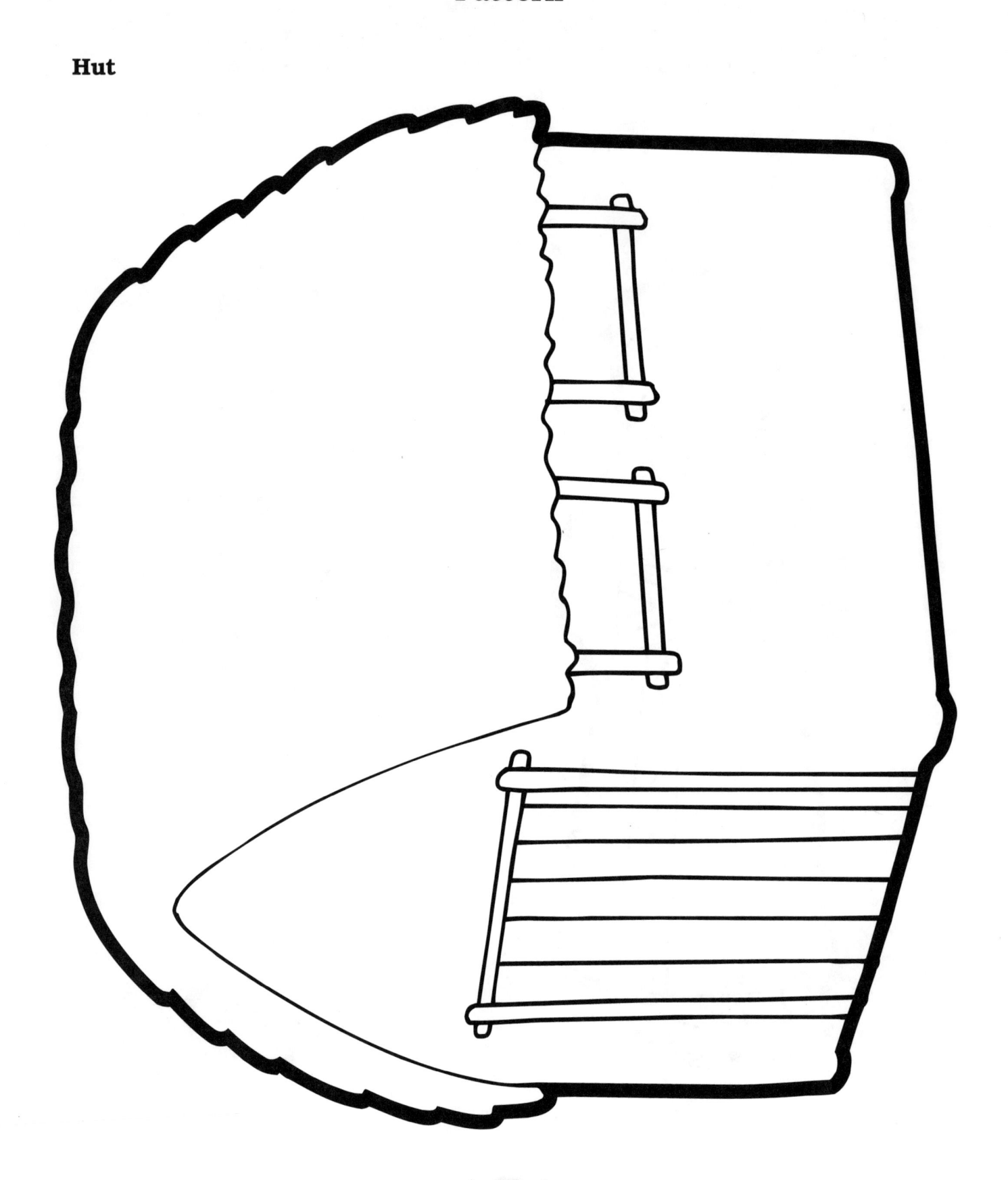

PRINCESS PARSLEY
Pattern

Hut

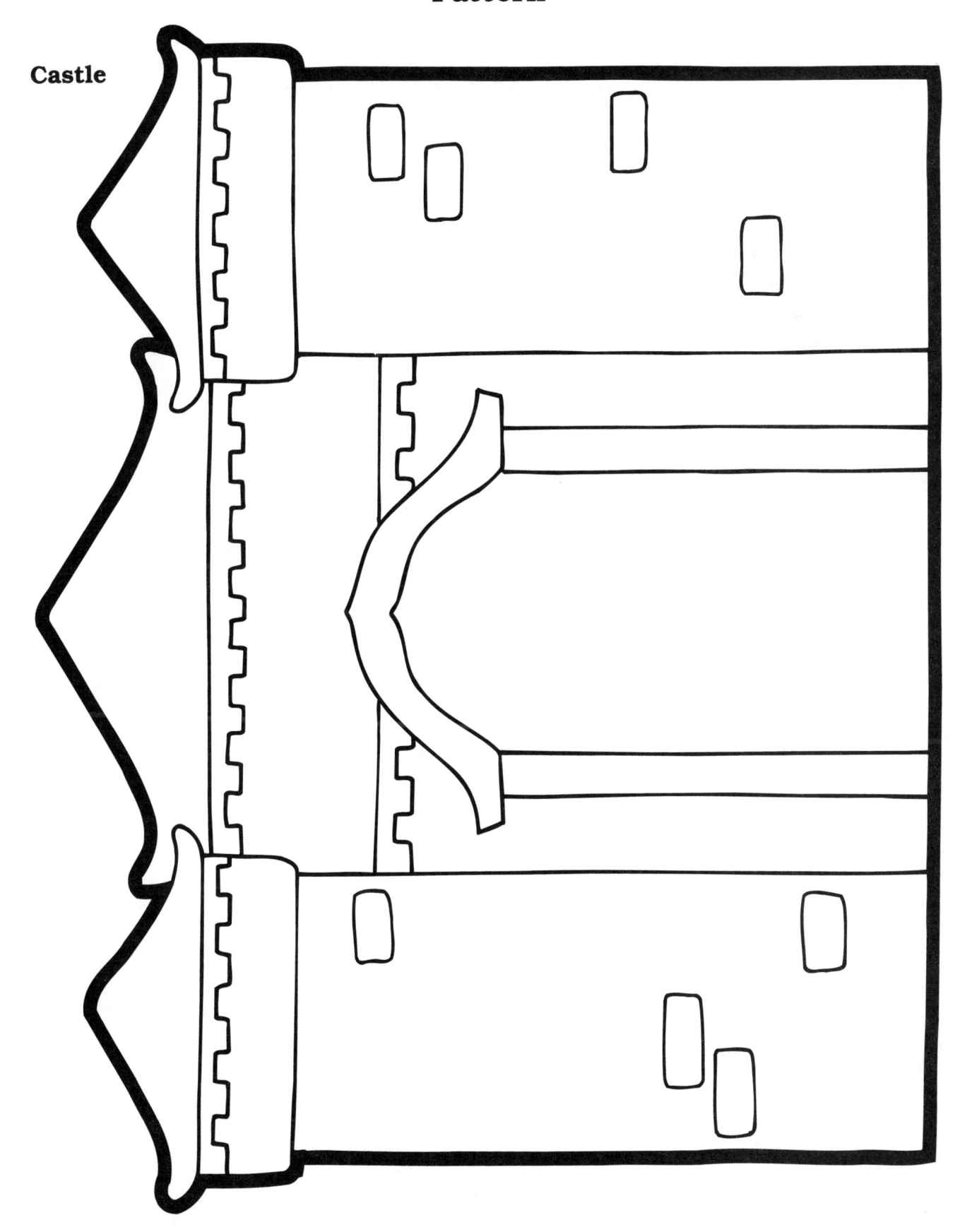

PRINCESS PARSLEY
Pattern

Castle

PRINCESS PARSLEY
Pattern

Big House

A THOUSAND LIGHTS FOR A KING
A Hindu Legend

Once there was a good king named **Dasrath**.
He lived in a beautiful **palace** in India with his son, **young Rama**.
Rama's mother died when he was just a baby,
And King Dasrath got married again so Rama would have a mother.
The **queen** had a **son** of her own,
And he and Rama played together like brothers.
But the new queen was a selfish woman.
She often thought to herself—
A wish, a wish, with just one wish
*For **gold**, for **silver**, I'd wish to be rich!*

Of course, she was rich, but not rich enough!
She didn't love Rama.
She wanted her own son to be king,
Because she thought she could make him keep all the riches.
She did not want to share like the good King Dasrath did.
One day, King Dasrath and the queen were in the garden.
King Dasrath was picking fruit high up in a **tree**,
And the queen was sitting on the grass daydreaming.
She thought to herself—
A wish, a wish, with just one wish
For gold, for silver, I'd wish to be rich!

Of course, she was rich, but not rich enough!
Suddenly King Dasrath lost his balance and began to fall.
The queen saw him just in time and threw out a **pillow**,
And the king landed safely in the middle of the pillow.
"Oh, dear queen!" he cried. "You saved my life!"
"I will grant you any wish!"
The queen thought to herself—
A wish, a wish, with just one wish
For gold, for silver, I'd wish to be rich!

Of course, she was rich, but not rich enough!
"Any wish at all?" asked the queen. "Any wish?"
"Well," said the king, feeling a little nervous, "I keep my word."
The queen saw her chance to get rid of Rama.
"All right then," she said. "Send Rama away—
Send him away for fourteen years!"
"But he's my son," said Dasrath. "In fourteen years he'll be king!"

"You said any wish! Send him away!"
And so Rama was sent away.
But the people of India never forgot him.
Every year, at the same time, they put out **lights**,
Thousands and thousands of tiny lights to mark his way home.
But the queen couldn't wait for her son to be king.
The queen thought to herself—
A wish, a wish, with just one wish
For gold, for silver, I'd wish to be rich!

Of course, she was rich, but not rich enough!
She thought Rama would never return,
And she felt sure that her own son would be king.
But each year the people set out the lights.
Rama went on many journeys,
And he grew strong, and brave, and handsome.
When fourteen years had passed, **Rama** headed for home.
But he had been gone so long that he had forgotten the way!
He searched and searched and then,
Off in the distance, he saw thousands of lights!
The people did not forget!
Rama ran toward the lights.
And soon he was home in his palace,
To hugs from his father
And cheers from his people.
Only the queen was unhappy.
She thought to herself—
A wish, a wish, with just one wish
For gold, for silver, I'd wish to be rich!

Of course, she was rich, but not rich enough!
The people had a great party, and Rama became the new king.
But the queen wandered off, grumbling about riches and wishes.
She was never seen again.
And every year, the people celebrated Rama's return
With festivals and games and thousands of tiny lights.
(But they don't put out lights for the queen!)

GET INTO THE ACT

✦ Have the children call out the refrain every time it appears in the story, saying it louder each time:
A wish, a wish, with just one wish
For gold, for silver, I'd wish to be rich!

✦ Give each child a sheet of black construction paper to decorate with globs of glue and gold glitter. They can hold these sheets up when you mention the "thousands of tiny lights."

✦ Make many copies of the tiny lights patterns. Flannel-backed pieces can be topped with foil, sparkly ribbon, or glitter. Each of the three times the "thousands of tiny lights" are mentioned in the story, let a few children place their lights on the flannel board. At the end of the story, the background will be covered with them!

LINK INTO LEARNING

Wish Upon a Star!
1. Ask the children to imagine that they have been given a wish. What would they choose?
2. Have the children draw pictures of their wishes on large paper stars.
3. Label their drawings and post them on a "We Wish for . . ." bulletin board.

Palace of Fine Hearts
Create a beautiful palace like the one in which the good and generous King Dasrath might have lived.
1. Find a large cardboard box (refrigerator and TV boxes work well) and cut a door in one side.
2. Let the children decorate the box with newsprint, butcher paper, wrapping paper, or tempera paint.
3. Provide paper plates cut in half to be glued to the top of the box for a "tile" roof.

LINK INTO LITERATURE

✦ *The Stonecutter* retold by Pam Newton (G. P. Putnam's Sons, 1990).
This ancient story, which also has Japanese and Chinese versions, is about a stonecutter who constantly wishes to be someone (or something) better than he is: a merchant, the king, a cloud, the wind, a mountain, and then, finally, a stonecutter! Unlike the queen in "A Thousand Lights for a King," the character in this story ends up happy to be himself.

✦ *The Magic Cooking Pot* retold by Faith M. Towle (Houghton Mifflin, 1975).
A poor man asks the Goddess Durga for help feeding his family, and the goddess answers his prayer. However, the man must encounter demons and other misfortunes before his luck can change.

THINK ABOUT IT!

In this story, Rama doesn't remember his way home. But the lights show the way. In Hansel and Gretel, the children leave bread crumbs to mark their way home. Ask the children if they have special ways to remember where they live. Are there any landmarks near their houses: light posts, street signs, hydrants, special trees, flower gardens, etc.

This is a good time for the children to be certain they know their home phone numbers and to review the information they would give to emergency personnel (name, address, phone number) if they got lost.

A THOUSAND LIGHTS FOR A KING
Patterns

King Dasrath

Young Rama

A THOUSAND LIGHTS FOR A KING
Patterns

Queen

Queen's Son

A THOUSAND LIGHTS FOR A KING
Pattern

Gold and Silver

A THOUSAND LIGHTS FOR A KING
Patterns

Tree

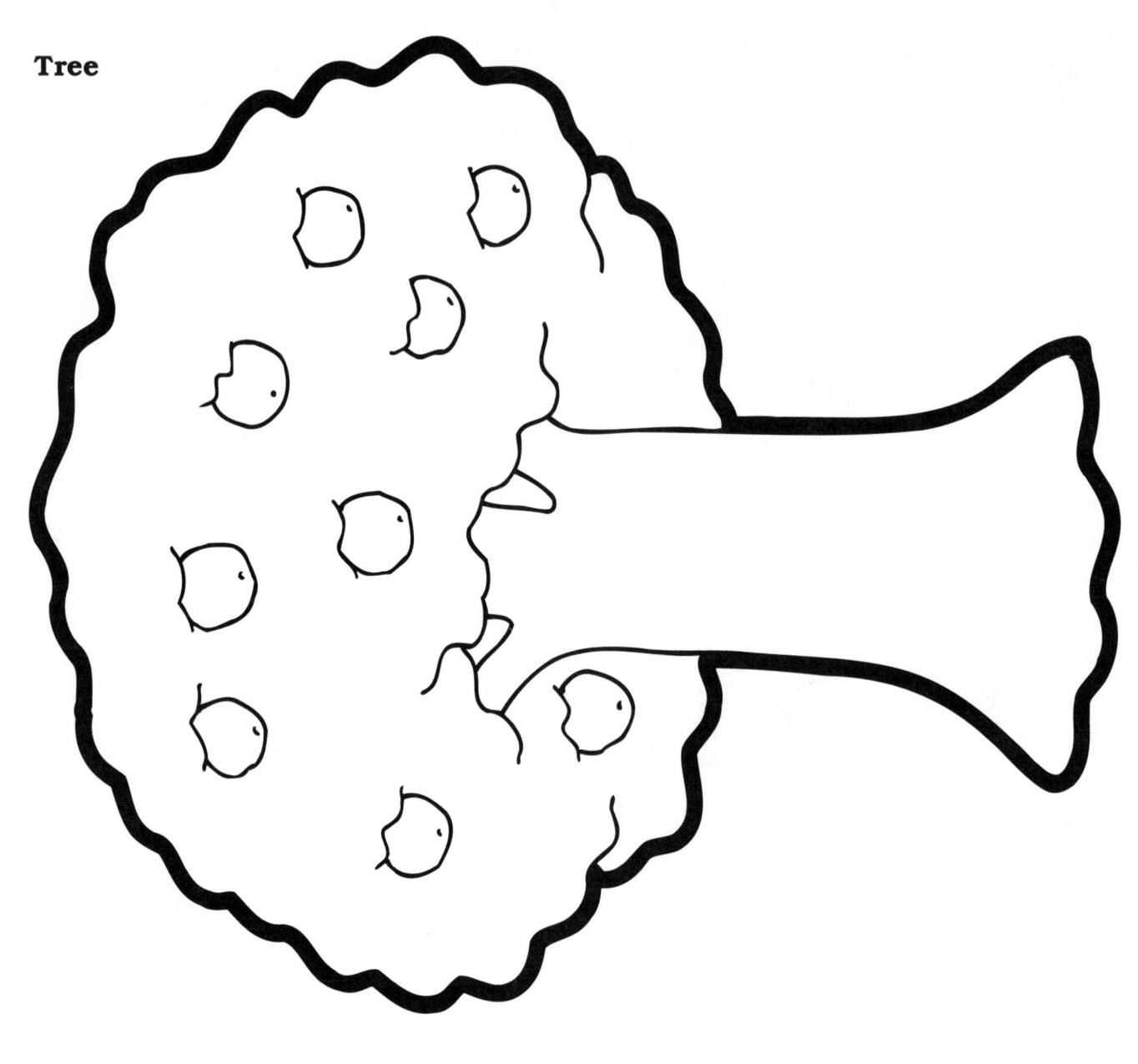

Pillow

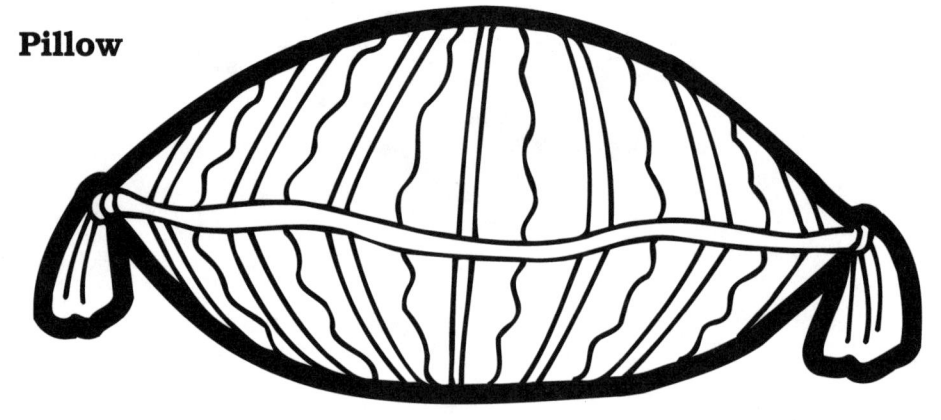

A THOUSAND LIGHTS FOR A KING
Patterns

Rama

Lights

A THOUSAND LIGHTS FOR A KING
Pattern

Palace

LITTLE JACK'S LANTERN
A Halloween Story Based on an Old Celtic Tale

Once upon a time, there was a little boy named **Jack**.
He liked to play tricks and scare people.
Every harvest season, when the **townspeople** were out at night
Celebrating, dancing, and sitting around the bonfires,
Jack would sneak through the bushes,
Low and quiet,
And shout, "BOO!" to the maid milking the cow,
"BOO!" to the baker kneading his bread,
"BOO!" to the farmer pushing his plow,
And "BOO!" to the carpenter building his shed.
Everyone would scream and yell,
And chase Jack back home.
Jack's mother would send him to bed early,
And Jack would go to **sleep** and dream the night away.
*He'd dream of **scary masks** and **sleek black cats**,*
***Ghouls and ghosts** and **pirates' hats**.*

And the very next morning,
Jack would be at it again!
He'd sneak around town,
Low and quiet,
And shout, "BOO!" to the maid milking the cow,
"BOO!" to the baker kneading his bread,
"BOO!" to the farmer pushing his plow,
And "BOO!" to the carpenter building his shed.
The townspeople would chase Jack back home,
And his mother would send him to bed early.
Jack would go to sleep and dream the night away.

He'd dream of scary masks and sleek black cats,
Ghouls and ghosts and pirates' hats.
And the very next morning,
Jack would be at it again!
But one morning, Jack thought up a new trick.
He went out to the pumpkin patch,
And he picked the biggest **pumpkin** he could find.
Then he hollowed out the pumpkin and put it on his head!
But there was one problem:
He couldn't see a thing.
So, Jack carved two triangles for eyes,

A big square for a nose,
And a great big circle for a mouth.
Then he put the **carved pumpkin** on his head again,
And set out for town.
He shouted, "BOO!" to the maid milking the cow,
"BOO!" to the baker kneading his bread,
"BOO!" to the farmer pushing his plow,
And "BOO!" to the carpenter building his shed.
This time, however, Jack had gone too far.
He had scared the people in town so much
That they were frightened to go out at night.
And that was the night of the big harvest festival!
So Jack and his mother thought up a plan
To make the townspeople realize that the pumpkin-head
Was only one of Jack's pranks.
His mother put a big candle inside the pumpkin to light the face.
Then the pumpkin looked more silly than scary.
That night, little Jack led all the townspeople
Out to the bonfire with his bright, smiling lantern.
Why, I guess you could call it a Jack-o'-lantern!
And at every harvest festival from then on,
Little Jack could be seen leading the crowd with his
    Jack-o'-lantern.
So, on the night before Halloween, when you go to bed,
Before you go to sleep and dream

. . . of scary masks and sleek black cats,
Ghouls and ghosts and pirates' hats,
Think of little Jack, whose trickery at harvest time
Is the reason we carve Jack-o'-lanterns.
Then go and find the biggest pumpkin,
And carve the silliest, scariest Jack-o'-lantern ever!

GET INTO THE ACT

✦ Have the children repeat the refrain when it appears in the story:
He'd dream of scary masks and sleek black cats,
Ghouls and ghosts and pirates' hats.

✦ Cut out a jack-o'-lantern face from a large paper bag. Paint the bag orange. Put the bag on with the face backwards to show how Jack felt the first time he wore the pumpkin. Then turn the face around so that you can see through the holes. Finally, take the pumpkin bag off and shine a flashlight through it to show how the candle looked in Jack's jack-o'-lantern (you might want to turn the lights off when you do this).

LINK INTO LEARNING

Shape-o'-lantern
1. Cut one round pumpkin shape from orange paper for each child.
2. Cut circles, triangles, and squares from black paper (enough so that each child can put together a face on an orange pumpkin shape).
3. Let each child make a shape-o'-lantern by gluing the black cutouts to their orange pumpkin.
4. Post the finished pumpkins on a pumpkin patch bulletin board.

Performance Piece
Have children act out the refrain to this story, taking turns playing Jack, the milkmaid, baker, farmer, and carpenter. Easy costume ideas: school clothes for Jack, an apron and a bucket for the milkmaid, jeans and a bandanna or straw hat for the farmer, a chef's hat and a rolling pin for the baker, and overalls and a play hammer for the carpenter. Other parts to add: the cow, a baker's assistant, the horse pulling the farmer's plow.

LINK INTO LITERATURE

✦ *Jack in Luck* adapted by Anthea Bell (Neugebaur Press, 1992).
This fun story is about another Jack, a happy (but not too clever) lad. Have the students compare the personalities of the two Jacks. Or talk about the not-so-wise trades that Jack makes. Ask the children how Jack might have solved his problems in other ways.

✦ *Jack and the Giant Killer: Jack's First and Finest Adventure Retold in Verse as Well as Other Useful Information About Giants* by Beatrice Schenk de Regniers (Atheneum, 1987).
Whimsical art combined with "giant lore," including the right way to shake hands with a giant, makes this book a must for any "Jack" unit!

✦ *The History of Mother Twaddle and the Marvelous Achievements of Her Son Jack* by Paul Galdone (Seabury Press, 1974).
This is a humorous and lively version of "Jack and the Beanstalk."

✦ *Jack and the Beanstalk* by Steven Kellogg (Scholastic, 1965).
Kellogg's classic illustrations (done in basic black and white with green additions) add a sparkle to the beloved tale.

THINK ABOUT IT!

Ask the children if they think that Jack did a safe thing by walking around with a pumpkin on his head. Use this question as a lead-in for a discussion on Halloween safety. Ask the children to suggest comfortable and safe Halloween costumes. Talk to them about reflector tape, flashlights, and crossing streets at nighttime. You might want to invite a police officer to the classroom to discuss safety further.

Discuss the different personalities of the Jacks in the various stories you read. Ask the children which Jack is most adventurous. Which one is smartest? Which would they like most for a friend? Have the children try to think of other Jacks they know from storybooks: Jack-be-nimble, Jack Sprat, Jack of Jack and Jill, little Jack Horner . . .

LITTLE JACK'S LANTERN
Patterns

Jack

Jack Sleeping

LITTLE JACK'S LANTERN
Pattern

Townspeople

LITTLE JACK'S LANTERN
Pattern

Jack's Mother

LITTLE JACK'S LANTERN
Patterns

Scary Masks

LITTLE JACK'S LANTERN
Pattern

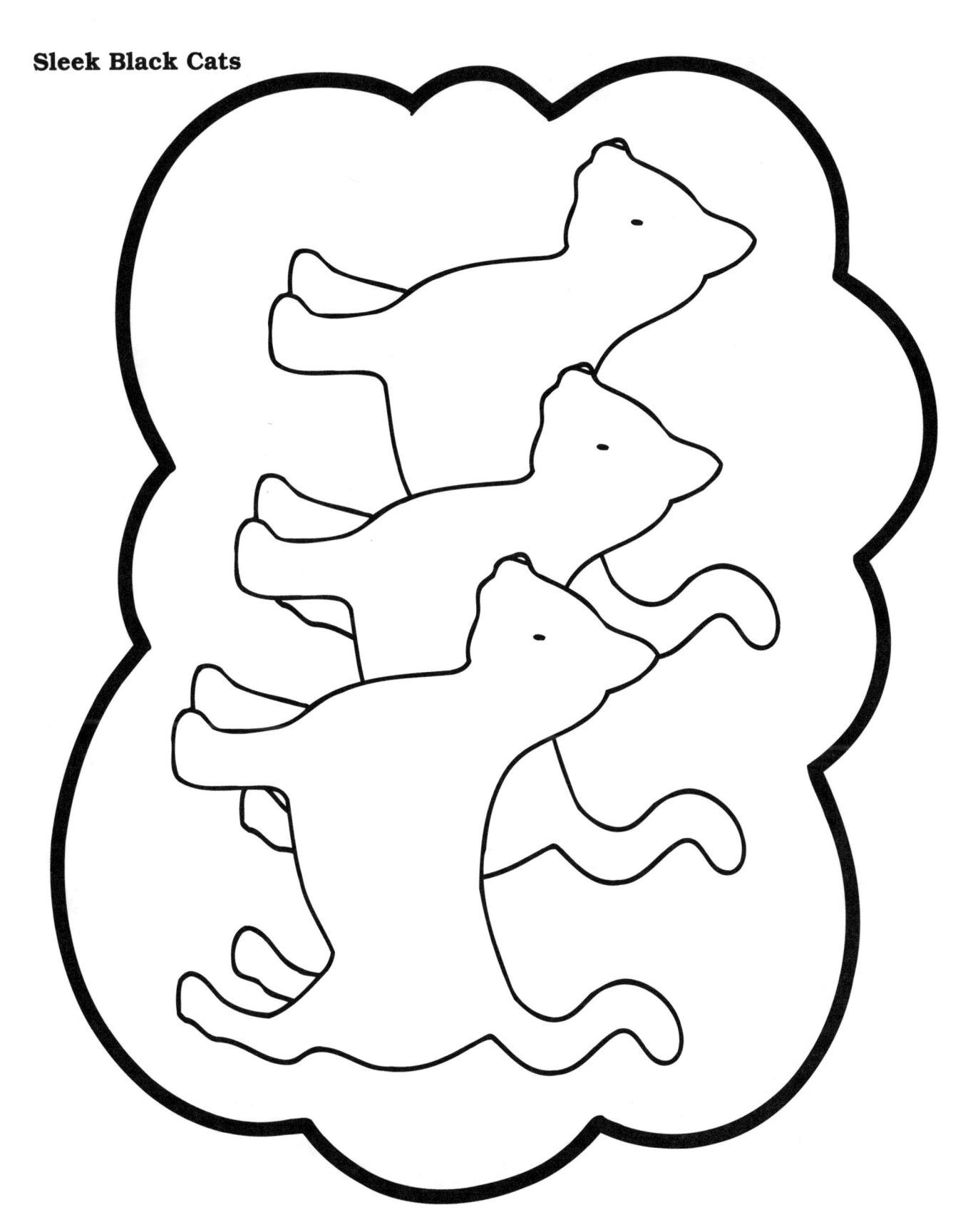

Sleek Black Cats

LITTLE JACK'S LANTERN
Pattern

Ghouls and Ghosts

LITTLE JACK'S LANTERN
Pattern

Pirates' Hats

LITTLE JACK'S LANTERN
Patterns

Jack-o'-lantern

Pumpkin

THE QUEEN OF HEARTS HAS A BIRTHDAY!
A New Story Based on the Traditional English Rhyme

Once upon a time, or so the folks say,
The young **Queen of Hearts** had quite a birthday!
All of her family, and all her friends, too,
Decorated the **castle** with ribbons of blue.
They brought presents and hats and red candy hearts,
And off in the kitchen, the **king** baked the **tarts**.
And he sang to himself as he baked through the day,
Because singing can help pass the time away,
"I'm baking tarts for my lovely queen,
The prettiest tarts she's ever seen,
They're small and sweet and good to eat,
These sugar-coated, heart-shaped treats."

In the ballroom, the Queen was alone
She thought of her party, and sat on her **throne**.
She counted **balloons** hanging over her head.
One blue one, two green ones, three yellow, four red.
She looked all around, but did not see a cake.
What's a party without one, for goodness sake?
But the queen didn't mind, as she looked about,
She didn't frown and she didn't pout.
Instead, she sang to help pass the time,
Her song was a lot like the king's own rhyme.
"I'm waiting for tarts, baked right for a queen,
The prettiest tarts I've ever seen.
They're small and sweet and good to eat,
Those sugar-coated, heart-shaped treats."

The castle was decorated for a huge party,
And the **guests** hurried, so as not to be tardy.
They cleaned and pressed their party clothes.
They wrapped their **presents** and fastened their bows.
But the **Knave of Hearts** wasn't feeling excited.
His mailbox was empty—he wasn't invited!
The castle mailman had forgotten the knave,
And since his feelings were hurt, he didn't behave!
So he went to the kitchen where the king was cooking.
He crept inside and started looking.
And he sang a song as he looked around,
He sang it softly, making barely a sound,

"He's baking tarts for the birthday night.
I'm going to take them clear out of sight.
They didn't invite me—and I'm feeling mean.
I'll take those tarts—baked for the queen.
They're small and sweet and good to eat,
Those sugar-coated, heart-shaped treats."

The knave ran inside and picked up a tray.
He stole those tarts and took them away.
When the king saw what the knave had done,
He threw down his **apron** and started to run.
He chased the poor knave up one hill and down,
He chased the poor knave all over the town.
The race went on, but it was getting late.
The king almost caught up in front of the gate,
But the knave ran ahead, straight into the castle.
There was yelling, and screaming, oh, what a hassle.
Before the knave knew it, he heard the door slam,
He'd run into the ballroom—he was caught in a jam!
But all of a sudden, the queen saw the tarts,
(And you know they're a favorite with the Queen of Hearts).
She shrieked in delight when she saw the tray.
She said, "Thank you for coming to my party today!"
The knave said, "I'm sorry I stole and was bad,
But I wasn't invited, and it made me so mad!"
"Poor boy," said the king, "it was all a mistake.
Of course you're invited—now come help me bake!
Let's go to the kitchen. We need some more tarts!"
And off the two went, the two men of hearts!
And the queen and her guests, well, they started to sing—
As the great birthday bells started to ring.
They sang, "Bring us the tarts that are fit for a queen—
The prettiest tarts that anyone's seen.
They're small and sweet and good to eat,
Those sugar-coated, heart-shaped treats!"

GET INTO THE ACT

✦ Practice the refrain with the children so that they can sing it together when it appears in the story:
*"They're small and sweet and good to eat,
Those sugar-coated, heart-shaped treats!"*

✦ Have the children make balloons out of felt to add to the flannel board. They can cut circles or ovals of different colors of felt and then glue a piece of string or ribbon to each one. Encourage them to name the colors as they press the balloons onto the board. You can have them make the appropriate number of balloons for each color mentioned in the story.

LINK INTO LEARNING

Tasty Tarts
1. Help the children roll out sugar cookie dough (pre-made cookie dough can be found in the refrigerator section of most grocery stores).
2. Let the children use heart-shaped cookie cutters to cut out a number of cookies.
3. Bake the cookies according to the decorations on the package.
4. Provide strawberry jam for the children to spread on their cookies before eating.

Tea Time
1. Set up a tea party on a picnic blanket spread in the center of the room. You can use plastic tea sets and have an imaginary tea. Or serve luke-warm tea with plenty of milk and sugar in paper cups.
2. Invite the children to bring a stuffed toy from home to join in the fun.
3. Ask the children to tell about their favorite birthday memories.

Mobile Magic
1. Paste two large red paper hearts back to back over a coat hanger, leaving the hook exposed for hanging. Make one for every three children.
2. Give each group of three a copy of the king, queen, and knave patterns to color.
3. Punch a hole in each pattern.
4. Thread a length of yarn through each hole and connect the patterns to the hearts with tape. Hang the mobiles around the room.

LINK INTO LITERATURE

✦ *The Real Mother Goose* illustrated by Blanche Fisher Wright (Checkerboard Press, 1993).
A great comprehensive selection of the best-loved Mother Goose rhymes. Have children take turns reciting the simpler rhymes, or acting out the more complex ones.

✦ *Catch Me & Kiss Me & Say It Again* by Clyde Watson (Philomel, 1992). This wonderful book is filled with variations on everything from counting rhymes to "This Little Piggy."

✦ *There Was an Old Woman Who Lived in a Glove* by Bernard Lodge (Whispering Coyote Press, 1992).
Though it starts out sounding familiar, this unusual story is actually quite original.

THINK ABOUT IT!

Ask the children what they think the king might have said to the knave to stop him from stealing the tarts in the first place. Why do they think the knave's feelings were hurt? Can they think of a better way for the knave to have expressed his feelings? Ask the children how they act when their feelings are hurt.

Ask the children what kind of present they would bring if they were invited to the queen's party. Have them draw a picture of their imagined gift.

THE QUEEN OF HEARTS HAS A BIRTHDAY!
Pattern

Queen of Hearts

THE QUEEN OF HEARTS HAS A BIRTHDAY!
Patterns

King of Hearts

Apron

THE QUEEN OF HEARTS HAS A BIRTHDAY!
Patterns

Tray of Tarts

Presents

THE QUEEN OF HEARTS HAS A BIRTHDAY!
Pattern

Throne

THE QUEEN OF HEARTS HAS A BIRTHDAY!
Patterns

Balloons

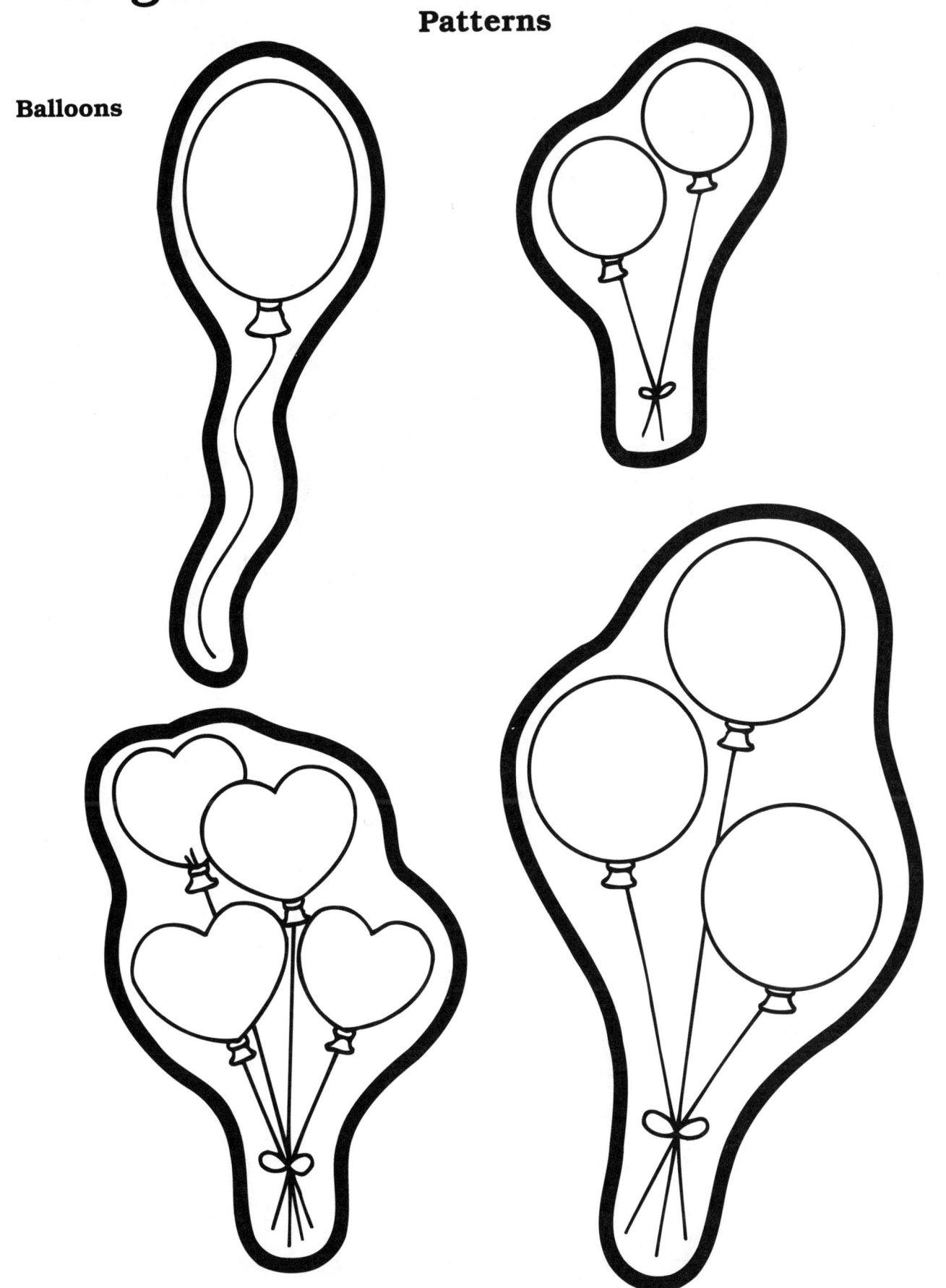

✦ 111 ✦

THE QUEEN OF HEARTS HAS A BIRTHDAY!

Pattern

Castle

THE QUEEN OF HEARTS HAS A BIRTHDAY!
Pattern

Guests

THE QUEEN OF HEARTS HAS A BIRTHDAY!
Pattern

Knave of Hearts

THE WISE BOY AND HIS DONKEY
A Tale from the Hispanic Southwest

There once was a young **boy** named Pedro who lived with his **mother**.
They were happy together in their little hut.
But as the boy grew older, he longed to go out on his own.
One morning, the little boy put on his warmest clothes.
"Mama, Mama, here I go," he told her.
"Wait, wait, my son, for another snow," his mother answered.
"You are too young to go this day."
So the little boy agreed to wait for another year.
The spring arrived with cactus blooming,
The summer burned with a blazing sun,
The fall blew in with chilly air,
And once the wintry nights had come,
The boy got ready to leave.

"Mama, Mama, here I go," the little boy said.
"Wait, wait, my son, for another snow," his mother answered.
"You are too young to go this day."
So the boy (who was bigger now) agreed to wait for another year.
The spring arrived with cactus blooming,
The summer burned with a blazing sun,
The fall blew in with chilly air,
And once the wintry nights had come,
The boy got ready to leave.

His mother led the boy's **donkey** to his side.
She put a thick warm poncho over his shoulders.
She gave him a package of meat and bread, and said,
"Now you are tall, and strong, and smart,
So you must go. But promise to return before the next snow."
The boy promised, and set out along his way.
He rode for miles until he met a smiling **woman**.
She was clothed in a long blue robe.
The boy had never seen her before, but she knew him by name.
"Pedro," she said. "Come near.
There are many strangers on this road," she told him.
"You must be careful and wise."
Then she handed him three delicious-looking red **apples**.
"When you meet someone, cut an apple in half to share.
If the stranger grabs for the larger piece,
Be careful and stay aware."

Pedro put the apples in his poncho, thanked her, and rode away.
That night, he met a **stranger** who asked to share his fire.
Pedro cut an **apple** in **half** and offered it.
The man quickly grabbed the largest half,
So Pedro only pretended to go to sleep that night.
And sure enough the man got up and tried to steal his donkey!
Pedro jumped up and sent the man away.
The next day, Pedro met a **second man** on the road.
The man seemed tired and hungry,
So Pedro cut an apple in half, and offered to share it.
This man took the largest half, too.
So Pedro sat down for a rest and pretended to sleep.
And sure enough, the man tried to steal his donkey!
Pedro jumped up and sent the man away.
The next day, Pedro met a **third man** on the road.
He walked along with Pedro for awhile.
And that night he asked to share Pedro's fire.
At supper, Pedro cut an apple in half and offered to share it.
The man quietly took the smaller half,
So that night Pedro slept soundly.
But when he woke up in the morning his donkey was gone!
Pedro jumped up and raced all around,
But there was no sight of the man or his donkey.
Finally, he went sadly down to the river to wash.
And there was the man with his donkey!
The man was being helpful and kind—
He had led Pedro's donkey to the river for a drink.
From that day on, Pedro and the man were good friends.
They traveled together and found work on a ranch.
They worked together through the seasons.
The spring arrived with cactus blooming,
The summer burned with a blazing sun,
The fall blew in with chilly air,
And once the wintry nights had come,
Pedro got ready to leave.

And he returned to his mother before the first cold snow.

GET INTO THE ACT

✦ Have the children learn the refrain to repeat with you when it appears in the story. They can act out the verse while they say it with the following motions:

The spring arrived with cactus blooming,
(Make bursting motions with hands—opening and closing fists.)
The summer burned with a blazing sun,
(Wipe forehead as if sweating from the intense heat.)
The fall blew in with chilly air,
(Puff out cheeks and pretend to blow like the wind.)
And once the wintry nights had come,
(Shiver with cold.)
The boy got ready to leave.
(Pretend to pack a suitcase or put on a jacket.)

LINK INTO LEARNING

Apple Puzzle
1. Make several copies of the apple pattern on different colored paper or oak tag.
2. Cut the apple patterns in half with a jagged line (like a puzzle piece).
3. Mix all the apple halves together and let the children try to put the apples back together. (The same-colored pieces will match.)

Popsicle Puppets
1. Give each child a set of pattern pieces to color and glue to Popsicle sticks, making sure that an inch or two of each stick remains at the bottom to use as a handle.
2. Let the children stand the Popsicle sticks in small pieces of clay.
3. The children can use these Popsicle Puppets to act out the story as you read it.

LINK INTO LITERATURE

✦ *The Sleeping Bread* by Ed Czernecki and Timothy Rhodes (Hyperion, 1992).
This Mexican folk tale tells the story of Beto, who befriends a poor man. The book can be a wonderful entry into a discussion of social issues (the homeless and the less fortunate).

✦ *The Rooster Who Went to His Uncle's Wedding* by Alma Flor Ada and Kathleen Kuchera (G. P. Putnam's Sons, 1993).
This colorfully illustrated Latin American folk tale has great opportunities to work on sequencing and memory recall.

THINK ABOUT IT!

In "The Wise Boy and His Donkey," the boy must grow up before venturing into the world. He must be smart enough to take care of himself. Ask the children to think of different skills they must master before they will be considered grown-ups. Ask if they can name the skills they have already learned (tying their shoes, counting to ten, knowing the ABCs, making their beds, etc.).

THE WISE BOY AND HIS DONKEY
Pattern

Pedro

THE WISE BOY AND HIS DONKEY
Pattern

Pedro's Mother

THE WISE BOY AND HIS DONKEY
Pattern

Donkey

THE WISE BOY AND HIS DONKEY
Pattern

Woman in Robe

THE WISE BOY AND HIS DONKEY
Patterns

Apple

Cut Apple

THE WISE BOY AND HIS DONKEY
Pattern

First Man

THE WISE BOY AND HIS DONKEY
Pattern

Second Man

THE WISE BOY AND HIS DONKEY
Pattern

Third Man

RESOURCES

More Folk Tales

Aardema, Verna. *Bringing the Rain to Kapiti Plain.* New York: Dial, 1983. (African)

Aardema, Verna. *Why Mosquitoes Buzz in People's Ears.* New York: Dial, 1976. (West African)

Ata, Te. Adapted by Lynn Moroney. *Baby Rattlesnake.* San Francisco: Children's Book Press, 1989. (Native American)

Birdseye, Tom. *Soap! Soap! Don't Forget the Soap!* New York: Holiday House, 1993. (Appalachian)

Bishop, Claire Huchet and Kurt Wiese. *The Five Chinese Brothers.* New York: Sandcastle Books, 1989. (Chinese)

Climo, Shirley. *King of the Birds.* New York: Harper Trophy, 1988. (Found in Aesop's European, and Chippewa Indian versions)

Cole, Joanna. *Best-loved Folktales of the World.* New York: Doubleday, 1982. (International)

Ginsburg, Mirra. *The Chinese Mirror.* New York: Harcourt, Brace, Jovanovich, 1988. (Chinese)

Kimmel, Eric A. *Baba Yaga: A Russian Folktale.* New York: Holiday House, 1991. (Russian)

Lee, Jeanne M. *Toad Is the Uncle of Heaven.* New York: Henry Holt, 1985. (Vietnamese)

Mayo, Margaret. *Magical Tales from Many Lands.* New York: Dutton's Children's Books, 1992. (International)

McDermott, Gerald. *Zomo the Rabbit: A Trickster Tale from West Africa.* New York: Harcourt, Brace, Jovanovich, 1992. (West African)

McGuire-Turcotte, Casey A. *How Honu the Turtle Got His Shell.* Austin, Texas: Steck-Vaughn, 1992. (Hawaiian)

Mosel, Arlene. *Tikki Tikki Tembo.* New York: Holt, 1992. (Chinese)

Retan, Walter. *Favorite Tales from Many Lands.* New York: Grosset and Dunlap, 1989. (International)

Taylor, C.J. *Little Water and the Gift of the Animals.* Montreal, Quebec: Tundra Books, 1992. (Seneca Indian)

Winter, Jeanette. *Follow the Drinking Gourd.* New York: Dragonfly Books, 1988. (African American)

Young, Ed. *Lon Po Po.* New York: Philomel Books, 1989. (Chinese)

Young, Ed. *Moon Mother.* New York: HarperCollins, 1993. (Native American)

Many more excellent illustrated folktales with specific links to the stories found in this book can be found in "Literature Links" at the end of each folktale.